Legends
of the Sea

Legends of the Sea

Text by
F. Morvan

Translated by
David Macrae

Crescent Books
New York

First English edition published by
Editions Minerva S.A., Genève.
Copyright © MCMLXXX
by Editions Minerva S.A., Genève.
All rights reserved.

Library of Congress Catalog Card
Number: 79-57031
ISBN: 0-517-307073

This edition is published by Crescent Books,
a division of Crown Publishers, Inc.

a b c d e f g h
Printed in Italy

Contents

The origin of the sea

In virtually all the mythologies of the world, water is given primacy over all the other elements. It was the first thing, after which came all the others. According to the Greeks and the Aztecs, even the gods were born of water. The various cosmogonies go back no further than the period in which the waves of the Primeval Ocean rolled across a shoreless waste, under the eternal night sky.

The earth, the sun and the stars ware hidden in its bottomless depths. The ancient Mexican baptism formula said that we are all the sons of Chalchithui-tyene, the goddess of water. The Peruvians said the same about Mama Cocha, the Botocudos about Taru, the early inhabitants of Darien about Dobayba and the Iroquois about Ataensic—all of these deities being mothers of mankind, and personifications of water. In the Oceanian legends, the sea alone existed at the beginning of time. Before the creation of the universe, in the opinion of the Kalmuks, there was nothing but an immeasurable abyss. From the bottom of that abyss there rose clouds of gold which projected lightning and which melted into rain, thus forming the Ocean.

If one consults the theogonies of the earliest peoples of the ancient world one comes across the same ideas. In the Biblical tradition the waters existed before everything else: in the beginning (Genesis, I) the spirit of God moved upon the face of the waters. After creating light, God divided the waters which were under the firmament from those which were above it... He also said: "Let the waters under the heaven be gathered together unto one place, and let the dry land appear: and it was so. And God called the dry land Earth, and the gathering together of the waters, the Seas".

The *Manava Sastra* tells the story of the Creation in the same order as the Bible: the World was obscure and confused, as if in a deep sleep. God, existing by virtue of his own powers, manifested himself in five elements and scattered the darkness. By wielding his power, he produced first of all the waters, imparted movement to them by means of fire and created an egg, as brilliant as the sun, from which Brahma, father of all reasoning beings, emerged.

The philosopher Zeno held a view which was close to the Biblical tradition and, in particular, to the Hindu tradition. He thought that God, existing spontaneously from the beginning, had turned all material things into water by means of air.

A Muslim legend gives another version of the creation of the Ocean and the limits within which it was confined.

It was at the very beginning of time: God created the sea ; then, thinking of his finest creature, man, he set limits for the immense power of the Ocean.

Addressing the waters which already covered three quarters of the earth, occupy the vast space which I am giving to you, but respect that part which is to be covered with flowers and plants, so that man may live there, happy and contented on your shores. You shall reflect from your bosom the blue of the sky; with the noise of your storms you shall repeat the echo of my angry voice; through you men will recognize me and you shall be the sword of my glory."

The sea promised to respect that which God had placed outside its range; but gradually it came to repent of its promise; arrogant in its new power, it dared to defy the Lord and mock his orders. It raised its waves against heaven, violently stirred up its furious waters and flooded the land. Man was on the point of being destroyed when God came along and spoke. The sea, submissively, licked gently at the sands on the beach without daring to go further.

"You have disobeyed me, O Sea, you have been ungrateful towards your Creator; you deserve to be punished—you, in whom I had always thought I had an obedient and submissive child. Fool! you imagined you were strong enough to challenge your Master! You shall be made to understand your weakness and my strength."

12

God then created the mosquito, and clouds of the insect swarmed into the sky, filling it like whirlwinds of dust. He ordered them to spread out over the sea; within a moment the tiny creatures had swallowed it up, so that it was dry. God then spoke to the sea which was shut up inside the stomachs of the mosquitoes.

"Can you hear me, O Sea?"

"Yes", came the trembling reply.

"Do you recognize me as your Lord?"

"I recognize you."

God then commanded the mosquitoes to return the water which they had swallowed, and the sea filled its basins once more.

Ever since then it has never tried to rebel, to flood the land or to destroy man. But while it was in the mosquitoes' stomachs its waters acquired the salty composition which they have never lost, and which was to be a reminder of its offense. This legend is reminiscent of a passage from the Book of Job, ch. XXXVIII, verses 8-10.

In a legend from Upper Brittany, relating to the power of the moon over the sea, the moon swallowed it up, also to punish it, but spat it out immediately as it was too salty.

The Tupi Indians of Brazil had a legend in which, one day, the earth was submerged by a deluge of fire. Only one man was saved, because Monan removed him and took him to heaven. The man complained to the god that he no longer had anywhere to live. Then Monan took pity on him and sent to earth a deluge which extinguished the fire and, flowing from all directions, formed the Ocean, which was called *Parana*, or "the great waters".

In Tahiti it seems that the sea was formed by Oo-Manao, one of the marine deities, different from the thirteen others which presided over it.

According to other traditions, various parts of the human body were formed from the sea. One medieval text has the blood of Adam being thus formed.

Certain New World peoples had some very strange legends about the creation of the sea; here are two of them, one from North and one from South America. In the beginning of the world, according to the Hurons, "the land was dry and arid and all the waters were gathered under the armpit of a large frog, so that Iskeka could not get at them except with the frog's permission. One day he decided to free himself and his descendants from such bondage; so he made an incision below the armpit, and the waters flowed out in such abundance that they spread all over the world, ant that is how the rivers, lakes and seas came into being." The Indians of the islands of Vancouver thought that the origin of the sea dated back to a basket which, containing all the water in existence, was taken by a slave from the giant who owned it; as he was being chased, the slave dropped the water, the greater part of it, heated by his sweat, forming the sea.

An Indian legend set to verse by Mello Moraes claims the following origin for the sea: Yaya had placed the mummy of her dead son inside a pumpkin and had abandoned it. Next day he saw enormous fish coming out of the pumpkin. Four twins came along and put the pumpkin on their shoulders; the liquid was oozing; Yaga appeared, whereupon the children, in their fright, ran away and dropped the pumpkin which, breaking open on the ground, flooded the most remote homes. And this, according to the primitive myth, was how the seas were created.

The earth, child of the sea

Most traditions and cosmogonies relate that, at the beginning of time, the water contained the seeds of everything and that, in particular, the earth was covered by the waves, awaiting the creative agent which was to make it rise above them.

In the *Kalevala* (first runo), the virgin Luonnotar descended from heaven into the sea which made her fertile, and for seven centuries she swam about on the boundless waves. One day she lifted her knee above the water, and an eagle came and laid its eggs on it; six of them were of gold, the seventh of iron. On the third day they fell into the sea because the virgin moved her knee; their lower part went to form the earth, the mother of all beings, while their upper part formed the sublime heavens, the sun being yellow, the moon white, the stars silvery specks ant the clouds black patches.

The New World legends which had the earth emerge from the sea by means of an agent, usually an animal, are very numerous. Here are some of them:

The Chipiouyans thought that the earth had once been nothing but a vast Ocean and that the only living being in the whole universe was a powerful bird. Its eyes were made of fire, its glances were flashes of lightning and the motion of its wings made a noise like thunder. It flew down to the Ocean and, as soon as it touched the water, the earth rose above the waves and remained there, in balance.

According to the legend of the Quiches, in the beginning there was nothing but darkness and the silent sea. Then the hurricane passed overhead, and the solid earth appeared.

The Muscogees thought that before the creation there was only a huge expanse of water, over which two pigeons flew. Eventually they picked up a blade of grass floating on the water. The dry land gradually made its appearance and the islands and the continents occupied the places in which they are now situated.

The Hurons had a story in which the earth, at the beginning of time, was covered entirely with water, with the exception of a small island which bore the hope of the whole of the human race—a single man whose sole company was a fox and a small animal like a weasel. Finding himself confined to such a small area, the man invited the fox to dive into the water to see how deep it was; but the fox darted back out again, no sooner had it got its paws wet. The man kicked it back into the water, where it drank more than its fill. The other little animal, prompted by the man, dived in and hit the bottom, coming back with its snout covered in mud. By digging about on the bottom it brought back enough mud to make huge areas of fertile fields on land."

One comes across, in ancient civilizations, the notion of the earth floating on the water. Thales said that the earth was held up by the water on which it floated like a boat, and that the mobility of this support accounted for the fluctuations known as earthquakes.

According to the Edda, the earth will drown in the Ocean when time comes to an end.

Scandinavian mythology mentions a second period after the first destruction o the universe: a new, perfectly beautiful earth will then emerge from the ocean, producing fruit with no human intervention.

Another tradition has the sea dying of its own accord; the Siamese believe that when the time comes for the world to end, the seven eyes of the sun will open in the heavens and gradually dry up every single thing. The fifth eye will be the one that dries up the sea.

The names of the sea

Among the two or three thousand languages which, at a conservative estimate, are in use in various parts of the world, there can scarcely be one which does not have one or more terms to designate the prodigious mass of water which surrounds the continents and forms the great trade routes between the nations.

It is true that there are tribes which live inland, away from the coasts, but it is rare for those furthest removed from the sea to be unaware of its existence. A catalog of names of the sea would be a lengthy undertaking, difficult and of necessity incomplete.

As the sea is, *par excellence*, a huge object, it has been used with reference to many types of vast expanse, even of things other than liquids. In Asia Minor, for example, the largest forest in the region is known as the *sea of trees*, the great prairies of Texas are sometimes known as the *sea of grass*, and the desert a *sea of sand*.

The Sahara contains the "sea of palm-trees". A plateau in the Salzburg Alps is known as the *Steinernes Meer*, or sea of stones, just as some French glaciers can be known as *Mer de Glace*, "sea of ice".

The term *sea* has also been used figuratively to designate thoughts or abstractions: "The lion remained for a while plunged into a sea of different thoughts"; "lost in the immense sea of my own misfortunes, I cannot forget the details of my first shipwreck".

The popular imagination conferred upon unknown seas, or those where mariners dared not sail, certain strange properties and some highly significant names:

According to Pindar and Euripides, navigation became impossible as soon as one passed beyond the Pillars of Hercules. Tacitus has the following to say about two seas of Northern Europe where traffic was extremely light in his day: "Reports say that this sea, which is situated to the north of Brittany, is slow and lazy under the oar, and that the winds to not stir it up as they do elsewhere. Beyond the Suiones is another sea, which is dormant and almost completely motionless. It is thought to be the belt and the outer limit of the world, because the last light of the setting sun lasts there until the sun rises again next day."

Norman sailors used the term *Libersee*, or viscous sea, to describe the area around the Orcades, because of the frequent fog. The Arctic Ocean was named by the Scandinavians *Dumslaf* (dumb sea) and *Trollbotin* (enchanted gulf). The White Sea used to be known as *Gandvik* or gulf of prodigies.

A German proverb refers to a qualification applied to the Germanic Ocean because of the dangers which lay in wait for mariners there:

Nord-See, Mord-See
North Sea, Sea of Death.

The Atlantic Ocean, which was for many centuries quite unknown, held many fears for the navigators of antiquity and the Middle Ages, as can be seen from the names which were given to it.

Carthaginian sailors used to say that beyond Cerne the South Atlantic Ocean was rendered impassable by seaweed. Saint Amaro, a medieval figure, also found his course blocked by grass in the Western ocean.

The Arabs call the Ocean *Bahr al Modhallam*, the dark and gloomy sea. This epithet applies particularly to the Atlantic Ocean, because, in the words of Ebn Al Vardi "nobody knows what lies beyond it". For the same reason it is still known as *Baharel-Zolmat*, or sea of darkness. When the Arabs first ventured on to the ocean they were afraid; they visualized it as a place of darkness, covered with thick water through which it was impossible to navigate. Edrisi refers to the oceans in much the same terms as were used by Eschylus: "Its waters are thick and dark. The waves rise up frighteningly, and the water is extremely deep, the darkness is continual, navigation is difficult, the winds impetuous".

Hesiod also used the notion of darkness in his descriptions of the sea.

While most of the names given to the sea are abstract, this is not true of the many nicknames which are used to designate it. Some of these, in fact, are highly expressive, evoking ideas of animism and anthropomorphism. Some of them derive from comparisons inspired by the similarity between certain conditions at sea and familiar terrestrial objects.

On the Breton coast, the use of the word *eau* is in itself sufficient to denote the sea. This is true in Scotland also.

In Brittany it is known as the "great fountain", the "inexhaustible source" —a term also used by Homer *(Odyssey, I* and VII)—and also *le grand étang,* the big pond; this latter term is much used in Upper Brittany and was common in the 17th century.

On the Galician coast the sea is known as *el charco,* the pond or the pool; it is also said to be *como una poza,* like a pool.

Similar nicknames occur in Scotland, where the sea is sometimes known as the Haddock Peel (Pool), the fishtank, or the cod pond. "To send someone to the herring pond" is to banish him.

Other nicknames for the sea are: the Great Basin, and the Great Pot, in various languages.

In Upper Brittany the sea is known as the *grand pré,* or big meadow. This is an old expression; Cicero, in his translation of the *Phenomena* of Aratus, speaks of ships which cut with their bows the prairies of Neptune: *Rostro Neptunia prata secantes.*

It recurs in Basque; to express the notion of a rough sea one says: "there are sheep on the meadow" *(Sorho peza handia).*

In Basque the sea is nicknamed *Landa-Lihoa,* or "field of flax". In this respect the following anecdote is told: two women who were one day by the sea thought that they saw a field of flax at their feet and exclaimed: "Oh! what a magnificent field of flax!" The undulations of blue flax do, in fact, suggest such a comparison quite easily.

In a number of popular stories one hears of people who, on seeing a large field of flax in bloom, blue like the sea, the flowers undulating in the breeze like waves, exclaim that it is the sea and bathe in it.

When the sea is calm it is given graceful epithets. In almost all languages it is said to be beautiful. In Brittany, if it is almost without a ripple it is called a "bed of roses".

In Upper Brittany, when it is slightly rough, one says that the weather is "ladies'" weather; in Portugal a similar expression is used: *mar de senhoras*.

The sea, when calm, has been likened to a lamb. In Upper Brittany they say: "The sea is mild as a sheep", while in Lower Brittany it is said to be as gentle as a lamb *(Mor habask e-c'hiz annoan)*.

In Scotland it is 'as quiet as a lamb' (usually written *lam*).

In this state, in which it resembles a white thing or milk—either really or by assimilation—the sea is called white: in Provence (Mistral) it is called "*Mar blanco*", and in Lower Brittany "*Mor gwen*". When it begins to calm down it is said to be whitened.

In Lower Brittany, if the sea is still it is compared to milk—*Mor sioul e-c'hiz al leaz*, (quiet as milk), while in Portugal they say *mar de leite*, sea of milk.

The very calm surface of the water has been compared to oil, a natural image which dow convey several of its aspects:

The sea is as calm as oil. (Lower Brittany).

La mar douco comme d'oli (The sea is as beautiful as oil; Martinique).

The sea is also said to be "as smooth as though oil had been poured on it."

The tendency to attribute to the sea the passions of an animate being is evident in many expressions:

It can sulk, become aroused, angry: it can be threatening, and can roar and sing. Some people have even compared it to an impassioned preacher.

It used to be common in poetic usage to say, of malicious persons, that they were born of the sea. This is the sense in which Catullus says *Quod mare conceptum spumantibus expuit undis?* (What sea conceived you and then threw you from its foaming waves?) And Tibullus: "You received life from neither the vast abyss of the sea not from the dreaded Chimera."

The sea has been called deaf, as has the shore, because the sound of the waves makes it impossible to hear anything else (Erasmus). The Romans used the term *aequore surdior*. This image recurs in Shakespeare: "High-stomached are they both and full of ire, In rage deaf as the sea, hasty as fire". (Richard II.)

Sometimes, to express the extreme turbulence of the sea, it has been called mad. Shakespeare, with reference to Hamlet, compared his madness to that of the restless sea; when the King inquires as to Hamlet's state, the Queen replies: "Mad as the sea and wind when both contend which is the mightier."

The sound of the sea has naturally given rise to the most epithets ,and comparisons. In Upper Brittany, if in rough weather the sea can be heard making a noise like a moan, it is said to shout while weeping *(brait)*. If it 'sings' on the beaches or at the foot of cliffs, it "brays like a donkey".

The Dutch use the expression *wilde Zee* with reference to the sea and compare it to a wild animal. On the coast of Brittany it roars like an unchained lion; and in Scotland the same saying occurs: "She is roarin' like a lion."

In *Les Travailleurs de la Mer* Victor Hugo wrote: "The wind was ready to blow, the wind was ready to roar".

Sometimes, by assimilation to a bull it bellows, as in Provence (Mistral), where they say *La mar bramo*. The sea is also said to tremble. Shakespeare, in his *Winter's Tale* (III, III), says: "I would you did but see how it chafes, how it rages, how it takes up the shore."

Just as in Upper Brittany, so also in Scotland the sea sings on the shore. On the shore of Moray Firth the fishermen call the sound of the waves the 'song of the sea'. In some parts of England, if a sort of moaning is heard along the coast, the local people call it the *calling of the sea*. This expression recurs in French: "This great majestic howling which mariners know as the call of the Ocean" (Victor Hugo, *The Toilers of the Sea*).

In Scotland, a certain sound made by the sea is likened to the tolling of the bells: the *knell*.

The color of the sea has also been a source of comparisons, and sometimes even of animism. In this way its varied aspects became, in the poetic mythology of the Greeks, nymphs of varied colors.

Among the Nereids *(Iliad)* who, in the Moeric poems personified the aspects of the sea, one was the Blue Nereid, another the Milky and a third the Green.

Blue is obviously one of the common epithets. In the Russian folk tales, in the *Kalevala*, the sea is generally called the blue sea.

Along the Breton coast it is said to be somber or black as an ink bottle. When the sea changes color it is said to have changed sheets: *Ar mor a chench liser*.

Mariners considered that the green hue of the sea is usually a sign of shallow water, and indigo blue indicates great depth.

The Ancients drew omens from any unusual color in the sea. Among the sinister omens observed in Brittainy, Tacitus refers to that of the 'blood-colored sea' *(Annales, XVI, 22)*.

Besides epithets referring to the destructive power of the ocean, there are others which depict the mariner's love for this terrifying element.

In a number of French folk songs the sea is described as *joli* (pretty). In the *Dialogue of the Shipwreck*, by Erasmus, the sailors who are caught unawares by the storm call it 'rich, beautiful and merciful', in order to placate its wrath.

Certain other epithets are, as it were, of a technical nature. One talks of the *swell* of the sea, of the *trough* between high waves; and one says that the sea is choppy.

Proverbs (1)

There are a large number of proverbs about the sea; some relate to the sea itself, while others deal with the wind, ships and navigation.

Come mare (like the sea); without an end (Italian saying).

The sea is like grief, you cannot see its edges (Russian).

A stone thrown into the huge sea in no way disturbs the surface, but easily stirs up the water in a well. (Saadi, *The Garden of Roses.*)

We shall pass, the earth and the sea will remain (Russian).

Pinvidik evel ar mor, rich as the sea (Tréguier, France).

As rich as the sea, (Basque country).

Nenti cc'e cchiu riccu di lu mari, nothing is richer than the sea (Sicily).

D'er mangt i marki og meir i sjoen. There are many things in the fields, but many more in the sea (Norwegian).

Helvede, havet og den gierrige faaer aldrig nok. The sea, hell and the miser never have enough. (Danish.)

My bounty is as boundless as the sea, My love as deep. (Shakespeare, *Twelfth Night.)*

The sea complains it wants water.

To stop the Ocean with one's hand. (Japanese: To attempt the impossible.)

Does the sea stop at the sight of a stream? (Tamil.)

He is building a bridge over the sea.

To piss into the sea and preach to it are both equally futile; the sea will not grow bigger and he will not benefit therefrom. (Ragusa.)

Wasser in das Meer tragen (German); *Water in de zee brengen* (Dutch).

Giving to a rich man is like pouring water into the sea (Ottoman).

Doing good to a base person is like pouring water into the sea. *(Don Quixote.)*

A drop of water does not make a sea.

Will the sea be filled by the dew that falls? (Tamil.)

Han lyver saa Bielkerne maa revne uder Loflet. Som skulde vel sige at der var ikke Vand i Stranden. (Danish: He lies so badly that the rafters of the attic crack, just like someone who claims there is no water in the sea.)

Naar kvinder fattes Svar paa Stand.

I vester-Hav da fattes Vand.

Danish: When a woman has no reply to make on the spur of the moment, the sea is about to run dry.

To ask in advance is to dig in the sea. (Turkish.)

Water always runs into the sea. (16th century.)

Ogni acqua va al mare, all waters go to the sea. (Tuscan.)

Alt Vand flyder til Strand, og Penge til den rige Mand. (Danish: All the water goes to the sea, and all the money goes into the rich man's pocket.)

Alle Vande löbe til Havet, dog bliver det ey fuldere. (Danish: All the waters go to the sea, yet it is not thereby made any fuller.)

All the rivers flow into the sea, yet the sea does not overflow. (Chinese.)

Havet sluger det faerske Vand i sig, og giver det salte fra sig. (Danish: The sea receives fresh water, yet the water it gives is salty.)

The sea refuses no river.

Follow the river and you will reach the sea.

Mare exhauris; exurere mare. (Latin, Erasmus: To exhaust the sea; i.e., to attempt some impossible endeavor.)

Moult a faire qui la mer a à boire. (Leroux de Lincy, 15th century: He who has the sea to drink has plenty to do.)

Propertius, when speaking of difficult tasks, said: *Tu prius et fluctus poteris siccare marinos.* (You would sooner be able to drink the seas dry.)

Quand avès begu la mar, poudès ben manja li péis. (Mistral: When one has drunk the sea one can eat fish; in other words, when one has suffered some great setback, others can also be endured.)

One of Sir Walter Scott's characters used an interesting proverbial notion when he said: "I have learnt to plow but only on the sea, and to reap only on the rocks".

He mä evel ar ar mor or garek. (Breton: He is like the sea on the rocks, a stubborn person.)

In the last century Lemierre once said: "Neptune's trident is the scepter of of the world", without realizing that he was in fact paraphrasing two ancient proverbs. They are:

Chi xe paron del mar xe paron de la tera, (Venetian: He who is master of the sea is master of the land).

Herre over Vandet, er og Herre over Landet, (Danish: Master of the sea and so master of the land).

The sea made man's soul, and the waves give him intelligence. (Finnish.)

A fool throws a stone into the sea, and a hundred wise men would not fish it out. (Russian.)

Hai fortuna, e jettate a mari.

Damni sorti e jéttami a mari.

If you were born lucky you can throw yourself into the sea. Make me happy and throw me into the sea.

Nasce fortunato iettete a mare, e lo mar te caccia fora, be born lucky, throw yourself into the sea and the sea will want none of you. (Naples.)

Give a man luck and throw him into the sea.

Has a storm set the whole sea in motion? (Tamil.)

Will the yapping of the fox reach the sea? (Tamil.)

Ignis, mare, mulier, tria male. (Latin, Erasmus: fire, sea, woman: three evils.)

Mari, focu e fimmini, Diu nui scanza, from sea, fire and woman, God save us. (Sicily.)

Evid ar mor bout traïtour, traïtouroc 'h ar merc'hed. (Finistère: However treacherous the sea may be, women are even more treacherous.)

Crede ratem ventis; animam ne crede puellis.

Namque est femina tutior undor fide.

Deliver your boat to the winds, but not your soul to young women. The seas are more faithful than the faith of a woman. (Cicero.)

Do not rely on the speeches of the mighty, nor the calm of the sea, nor the evening twilight, nor the word of a woman, nor the courage of your horse. (Ottoman.)

The sea is an unfaithful field. (Serbian.)

The further one is away from the sea, the less is one's grief. (Russian.)

He who has been on the seas has known fear. (Russian.)

He who has never been on the seas has never seen grief. (Russian.)

He that would sail without danger must never come on the main sea.

If you would learn to pray, go to sea. (Wisdom of Sancho Panza.)

Chio no navega, no sa cosa sia timor de Dio, (Venetian: He who has not sailed the seas knows nothing of the fear of God.)

Whoever has not been to sea has not prayed to God to the full. (Russian.)

When setting out for the wars, say a prayer; when going to sea say two prayers; and if you want to get married, say three. (Russian.)

Lauso l'Uba, tèn-te à l'Adre;

Lauso lo mount, tèn-te à la plano;

Lauso la mar, tèn-te à la terra.

Praise the north and stay in the south, praise the mountains and stay on the plain, praise the sea and stay ashore. *(Armana Prouvençau.)*

There was a similar saying in Latin:

Laudetur mare, sed teneantur littora. (Praise the sea, but stay on the shore.) There are similar expressions in many languages. For example:

Praise the sea, but in a foreign country. (Russian.)

Praise the sea, but when you are seated on the stove. (Russian.)

Beyond the sea there is gaiety, but it is foreign; here we have sorrow, but it is ours. (Russian.)

Es miou si raccoumanda ai ome en terra che ai sant en mar, (Nice: It is safer to rely on men on land than angels at sea).

Satius est pauperem in terra vivere quam divitem navigare, (Menander: It is safer to live a pauper on land than to be rich at sea.)

Nothing is more exposed to vicissitudes than the sea. (Tacitus.)

A cottage on land is worth more than the price of a castle at sea. (Lower Brittany.)

Bedre fattig paa Landet, end rüg paa Vandet; en Skilling bedre paa Landet ent ti paa Vandet. (Danish: It is better to be poor on land than rich at sea; one penny on land is worth more than ten at sea.)

Beter met een ouden wagen in de heide dan met een nieuw schip op Zee, (Dutch: It is better to be ashore with an old cart than at sea on board a brand new ship.)

Beter arm te land, dan rijk op Zee, (Dutch: It is better to be poor on land than rich at sea.)

If you are ashore, do not seek the sea. (Erasmus.)

26

Isassoak adarric es, (Basque: The sea has no branches to which one can cling.)

He who falls into the sea would cling to a serpent. (Turkey.)

A drowning man clutches at a straw.

A drowning man clutches at piece of moss. (Arabic.)

Lu mari e senza funnu, the sea has no ropes. (Sicilian.)

He wrongfully complains of the sea who twice suffers shipwreck.

Someone once said that his great-grandfather, his grandfather and his father all died at sea. His companion then said: "If I were you I would never go to sea. — Why? he replied; where did your ancestors die? — Where? In their beds, of course. — If I were you, I would never lie down in a bed."

Ann douar d'ar c'houeridi.

Hag ar mor d'ann duda listri.

The land to the peasants, and the sea to those who sail in ships. (Lower Brittany.)

A similar saying exists in Sicily: The sea belongs to those who sail on it, and the land to those who plow it.

Being on the sea, sail; being on the land, settle.

Mundu hurec diduri itsassoa, iguerica estaquiena ondarrera doa, (Basque: The world is like the sea, since those who cannot swim drown.)

It is not the sea which sends ships to their doom, but the wind. (Russian.)

Mare coelo miscere, (Latin, Erasmus: To mix the sea and the sky; proverbial hyperbole expressing deep turmoil.)

Mare quidem commune certo't omnibus. (Latin, Plautus: The sea belongs to everyone.)

L'omu a mari,

Zoccu fa oggi fa dumani.

Man and the sea, what they do today they will tomorrow. (Sicilian.)

Freshwater fish do not go to sea. (Chinese.)

The sea does not buy fish. (Turkish.)

You cannot sell the fish that are still in the sea. (Turkish.)

Sea water

There is an ancient belief that when the world was newly-created, sea-water was as sweet as that of rivers and springs. Tales from various countries offer supernatural explanations of how it later became salty.

Once there was a sea-captain who fell in love with a girl who lived nearby. He courted and married her because she was graceful, though poor. After the marriage the captain went back to sea. While he was away a local lord fell in love with the young woman and, being very powerful, took her away to his castle and forced her to marry him.

When the captain returned he was heart-broken when he heard what had happened, but as he could not force the wicked lord to return his wife to him, he went back to sea again. He was away for several years and on his next return he learnt that the sea had swallowed the lord's castle, and that everyone in it, including the lord himself, had drowned. The only person saved was the captain's wife, who immediately returned to his house. When he heard the good news the captain was beside himself with joy and hurried to meet his wife. They were very happy to see each other again. He asked her how it was that she was the only one to escape death by drowning.

"One day", she replied, "the sea rose and flooded the lands of the lord who held me against my will. Soon it reached the castle and began to batter against its walls. Wave after wave, each higher than a masthead, made the walls totter and fall. All in the castle were either buried under the ruins or drowned, and after the death of those wicked men the sea grew calmer and I was able to return here."

"As the sea has spared you", said the captain, "I must go and thank it for the favor it has done me."

He went down to the sea and said:

"O sea, during my last voyage you did me a great favor: a wicked lord had carried off my wife and married her against her will. You destroyed his castle and drowned him, letting my wife go free. I have come to thank you and to show my gratitude. Everybody wonders at your vast extent and your tides, o sea. Henceforth they will wonder at your taste as well."

The sea gave no reply but followed the captain, who led it into a land full of salt-mines. The sea covered the land and the salt-mines, and ever since those days has been salt to the taste. The sea thanked the captain, who returned to his own country to live happily with his wife. Who knows, if he has not died he may be living there yet.

In Upper Brittany people have long believed that the sea is salty because it washes around mountains of salt: it is salty throughout because its ceaseless movement distributes the salt evenly over all its vast extent.

A Norwegian tale, *The Magic Mill*, gives a different explanation. Once there was a mill which, if certain magic words were spoken, would grind out anything one wished. In the end it came into the hands of a sailor, who quickly took it on board his ship without finding out the magic words needed to make it stop. When the ship was on the open sea the sailor said: "Grind out salt, grind it quickly and well". And the mill poured forth salt. When the ship was fully laden the sailor ordered the mill to stop, but it kept on working because it would only obey the right magic words. The heap of salt grew higher and higher until finally the ship sank. At the bottom of the sea the mill is still, to this day, grinding out salt, which is what makes the sea salty.

According to one author, Frodi, the king of Denmark, came to visit Fiölnir, king of Sweden, and bought two big, strong slave-girls called Fenia and Menia. In those days there were in Denmark two millstones which were so huge that nobody could turn them. They had the power of grinding anything one wished. This mill bore the name of Grotti and had been given to the king of Denmark by Hengikiapr. Its new owner had his slave-girls grind out gold-dust, peace and prosperity. They were only allowed to stop work or go to sleep when the cuckoo ceased its song or when they sang themselves. Once they sang the Grottasavngr from the Edda and wished that before they finished an army might arrive to fight Frodi. That very night a sea-king called Mysing landed with his men, killed Frodi and carried off vast quantities of plunder. Mysing took Fenia, Menia and the mill with him and ordered them to grind out salt. . At midnight they asked if there was now salt enough, but he told them to keep on grinding. They worked on, but in a little while the overloaded ship sank to the bottom of the sea. A whirlpool formed around the millstones, and ever since the sea has been salt.

Around Tréguier sailors say that the sea is salt because of the many salt-ships it has swallowed up since the world began. It will become saltier and saltier as more salt-ships are wrecked in it.

According to an Indian legend there was once a little man called Agastea, who was no bigger than a man's thumb, but hale and strong. One day he was walking by the side of the sea, which in those days was still sweet. The sea teased him about his smallness, he took offense and in revenge gathered the whole sea in his hand and swallowed it as if it were no more than a drop of water. The angels were aggrieved and complained to him saying now badly-off they would be without the sea. Eventually they persuaded him to put it back, so he passed it in the form of urine. That is why it is salt.

In the Middle Ages and in the 16th century scholars thought that the sea was salt on the surface only and ceased to be so below a certain depth.

English and French mariners also used to think that the water at the bottom of the sea was salt-free. Basil Hall reports having heard sailors say that if one let down a well-corked bottle to a depth of a hundred fathoms, one could bring it up full of fresh water. The same belief prevails in Lower Brittany; in the Tréguier region it is said that on the open sea, far from the coast, sailors who have run out of drinking water can replenish their supply by letting down a bucket weighted with a heavy stone.

Pliny reports that one of the magi sent by Tiridates on an embassy to Nero refused to travel to Rome by sea because he did not think it right to pollute that element with all the unclean by-products of human beings. This belief, attested by Marco Polo in the Middle Ages, has persisted for a long time in certain oriental countries. Seneca says that it is the nature of the sea to cast up on the shore all impurities. It casts up corpses, marine growths, and wreckage from the depths, and its purgings take place not only when storms rage but also in the flattest calms. In Upper Brittany it is also believed that the sea purges itself during storms and that it casts back corpses.

Certain of the peoples of Oceania still believe in the superiority of salt water over that of streams or rivers. The religious practices of the Brahmins, too, include bathing in the sea. Chapter XXXII of the Dharmasindu says that one can bathe in the sea at full moon, at new moon and at other times except Fridays and Tuesdays. The translator adds a note to the effect that the pilgrimage to the Bridge of Rama includes bathing in the sea. Bathing at the time of an eclipse, particularly if in sea-water, has the effect of purging one's soul of all defilement. Bathing at solstices and equinoxes, at new and full moon and on the eleventh day of the moon has the same effect.

The custom of bathing to expiate sins was observed in classical times. It is also found in the Americas, and there are traces of it in the East right up to modern times. Catullus says of someone who has not expiated his sins: *Non genitor Nympharum abluit Oceanus.* The translator adds the footnote: "The Ancients used to bathe in the sea to expiate their sins."

The ancient Peruvians used to bathe in the nearest river and repeat these words: "O river receive the sins I have confessed this day beneath the sun. Carry them to the sea for ever."

Many years ago at Banyuls in the department of Pyrénées-Orientales men, and particularly men of middle age, used to go down to the sea in the early morning of Midsummer Day. There they would bathe in the seawater and dry themselves by basking in the rays of the rising sun.

In Naples, according to an ancient custom still observed in 1580, all the men and women used to go down to the sea and bathe naked late in the evening of Midsummer Eve. They believed that they were washing away their sins, like the people of classical times who bathed in the Tiber for the same purpose.

Saint Augustine condemned as a remnant of paganism the custom amongst Libyan Christians of going down to the sea to be re-baptised on Midsummer Day.

The idea of purification can also be seen in the ceremonial bathing which gives its name to the Madagascar New Year Festival. The Siamese also bathe at this time, and according to Sangermann the Burmese celebrate the New Year by throwing water at one another.

Cypriot women make a pilgrimage to the sea once a year, just as in the days when they used to celebrate the birth of Venus. The foam of the waves is no longer sacred to her, but the Cypriots still dip their hands in it as an act of piety. They say: "We have three patron saints venerated above all others—St. George, St. Lazarus and the holy sea."

The Moslem women of Sidon gather in a huge crowd on a cliff to play, sing and cast their sins on a Christian woman, if they come across one, or into the sea, if they cannot find a victim. They dance in a field where a holy man's tomb stands and then they go and bathe naked in the sea to purify themselves. This ceremony takes place on a Wednesday once a year. It is believed that this strange custom goes back to the remotest antiquity.

At the Zanzibar New Year festival the colored population carry out various ceremonies the night before, ending with mass bathing in the sea. On this occasion the women wear garlands made from a creeper known in the local language as the 'New Year herb'.

There are many other instances: on the coast of the Red Sea people used to wash in the sea after having kept vigil over a corpse. The women of Massoua, after having spent the night with a widow lamenting the dead man, would bathe in the sea the next day, decked out in all their finery.

Sea-water is often connected with marriages and funerals. At Rotouna, on the day of the wedding, the bride and groom are taken to the shore, where they walk into the sea. The bride lies down in the water while the groom washes her. Then the groom lies down in the opposite direction while the bride carries out the same ceremony. This takes place before a large number of witnesses, who sing as they stand in the water.

Some nations have the custom of deliberately drowning themselves in the sea to please the gods.

In Japan those who are most imbued with the love of Amida offer the god their lives and think nothing of drowning themselves to do the god honor. Some plunge into the water head first. Others are taken out into the middle of a river in a little boat appropriately decorated, have stones attached to their legs, waists and necks, then they throw themselves into the water to the sound of music. Their parents, relatives, friends and a number of bonzes are present at the ceremony. The Germani used to drown themselves in the same manner in honor of their gods.

Others simply gather on the shore while one of them speaks to his friends on the unimportance of death. After a month of this they go on board a boat, where they drink and make merry. The occasion ends with everyone throwing himself into the sea and sinking the boat by boring a hole in its hull.

By reason of its saltiness sea-water is thought to have certain beneficial properties.

On the coast of Brittany people believe that it makes the limbs supple, whereas sweet water chills them. Around Finistère and Morbihan they have the saying: "Sea water never gives you a cold." Sailors are firm believers in this. They say that if it did cause colds as sweet water does, people would never go on board a ship to be drenched most of the time. In Finistère people tell of instances where men have left the land with heavy colds, only to lose them as if by magic the moment the sea drenched them to the skin.

In Scotland it is widely believed that being wet by sea-water has none of the unpleasant consequences that would be caused by sweet water, and that if salt water were as bad as the latter, no fisherman would survive.

Around Tréguier it is believed that to warm onself in cold weather, one only has to jump in the sea.

Oexmelin, in his *History of the Adventurers*, writes that in the 17th century the Dutch believed that throwing sea-water over passengers crossing the line preserved them from the sickness they might catch from a change of climate.

The medical science of the classical period made frequent use of sea-water. Pliny gives a long list of the maladies it was used to treat. Some of these beliefs have survived amongst ordinary people to this very day.

It said in Upper Brittany that if one has a cold one should drink sea-water night and morning. After one day of this treatment one will be completely cured.

In Poitou it is believed that sea-water cures chronic bronchitis and that a glass of it taken on an empty stomach heals a sore throat. In the Andaman Islands they drinks sea-water to guard against a cough.

Near Tréguier local people purge themselves with sea-water each spring and fall. Before drinking the water they blow on it to remove all impurities and pour a little on the ground before drinking. This kind of libation is also performed by those who draw water from the sea for other purposes. For maximum effect, according to local beliefs, it should be taken when the tide is going out.

In Spain sea-water was once considered an excellent purgative drunk in the morning before lunch. As large a dose as possible was drunk, followed by water from a chalybeate spring. If this was not available, water from an ordinary spring was used.

Even in classical times seawater was given as a purge and to flush out black bile and clots of blood. "Some", says Pliny, "prescribe it for quartan agues and administer it, after it has long been kept in store and thus deprived of its unpleasant qualities, in cases of tenesmus and complaints of the joints. Others prescribe it boiled. All stipulate that it should be drawn from the open sea and free from an admixture of any sweet substance and that the patient should vomit before using it. It must in that case be mixed with vinegar and wine. Those who administer it in a pure form recommend that the patient also eat horse-radish with honeyed vinegar to facilitate vomiting. Seawater was also used as an enema."

To quote Pliny again: "Physicians find seawater an effective cure for tumors. Boiled with barley flour, it is used to cure aliments of the parotid gland. It also used to mix plasters, particularly white plasters and poultices. Nothing can surpass it as a fomentation for swollen testicles and for chilblains before they burst. Sea-water is also beneficial for itches and psoriasis. It kills nits and other head-vermin. It restores their natural color to those parts of the body which have become pale. It is also regarded as a treatment for stings and the venom of the ptyas asp, in which case it is used hot. Mixed with vinegar it makes an inhalant which cures headaches. The steam of boiling sea-water and vinegar is used to treat hearing problems and headaches. Heated sea-water is prescribed for nervous pains, to knit fractures, for bruised bones and also to dry out the body. For the latter purpose cold sea-water is also used."

An author of the last century writes that one day he saw a ship pass by with an old man tied to one of its yards. "I asked what was the meaning of the sight. One of the sailors replied that the old man was mad, having been bitten some time before by a rabid dog. I asked why he was taken down to the sea and whether the purpose was to kill him. The sailor said that the idea was to cure him, adding that the sea had the power to cure madness instantly." The author went aboard the ship to observe this curious treatment, which to judge from his description must have been rather like execution by drowning, for the patient was held under water for the time it took to say an Ave Maria, with the result that he appeared to be dead when taken out of the water."

In earlier days sea-water was much used as a remedy by peasants, sailors and even courtiers. In 1671 Madame de Sévigné wrote: "If you think the queen's maids of honor are mad, you are quite right. A week ago Madame de Ludres, Coëtlogon and the little de Rouvroi girl were bitten by a dog at Theobon. The dog has now died of rabies, with the result that Madame de Ludres, Coëtlogon and Rouvroi have this morning left for Dieppe to be plunged in the sea three times."

The Basques of former times used to believe in the effectiveness of sea-bathing as a cure for madness. In those days people did not go to the beach as they do today, in search of relaxation. If someone was suffering from madness they tied him on a horse and gave him an enforced plunge in the sea.

The old French proverbial expression for a madman, "a man fit to be plunged into the sea", probably contains an allusion to this custom.

This superstition was doubtless taken to America by English colonists. In

The Pilot by Fenimore Cooper one character tells another that if he is to be cured, he will have to be prescribed sea-water, as is sometimes done in cases of madness.

The taking of baths was even used to prevent unpleasant dreams. "If by chance you hear some nocturnal vision or if you have been suffering from the visitation of Proserpine" says Plutarch *(On Superstition,* III), "call the crone who kneads your dough and plunge into the sea."

The effectiveness of sea-baths depends on the time of the year when they are taken, on their number and on the state of the sea.

In Brittany it is believed that it is dangerous to enter the water during the dog-days, unless one has already bathed three times before then. To feel any real benefit one must bathe at least three times.

According to a Portuguese belief a sea-bath taken on St. Bartholomew's Day is worth seven at any other time. They must always be taken in uneven numbers.

In Asturias the ordinary people do not bathe on St. James's Day for fear of misfortune. It is believed that it is best to bathe while it is raining, as the rain tempers the sea-water.

In Scotland people bathe when the tide is coming in, thinking the sea-water to have maximum strength and effectiveness at that time. Bathing at low water or when the tide is going out is considered harmful to one's health, according to W. Gregor.

Some years ago it was the custom in some parts of Scotland to throw stones into the water before going for a swim. Some threw three stones of different sizes, starting with the largest. White stones were preferred, if they could be had. Other people used to throw stones into the water without regard to number, but repeated certain phrases.

Customs and beliefs concerned with swimming would provide the basis for some very interesting research.

Among the seagoing nations, especially those whose state of civilisation is not particularly advanced, the skill of swimming is almost as necessary as that of walking, and parents encourage children to learn to swim from earliest infancy. The inhabitants of the Pelew Islands teach their children to swim very early, both girls and boys. One can see mothers throw their children into the water as many as twenty times when the children are no more than two or three, watch them as they flounder and only take them out when they are on the point of drowning. In this way they learn to swim at a very early age and soon play about in the water like dolphins.

In Brittany the children of fishermen learning to swim tie a plank to their backs to support them in the water. When they have learned to swim they say proudly: "*Nous savons prendre l'eau à poignées*" ("We know how to take handfuls of water"). Then they play a great game of floating on their backs, imitating the corpses washed in by the sea.

They also imitate the movement of fishes and boats. When they swim up to a rock they repeat the cries of sailors, such as "Hard a-starboard!" They enjoy turning somersaults in the water, rather like porpoises or dolphins.

In Brittany and on the west coast of France generally fishermen think that jelly-fish are born from the excreta of the sea or from the poisons purged from it by the storms. The same belief occurs in Sicily.

According to Pliny anchovies are born from sea-foam whipped up by falling rain, and shell-fish from decaying mud or from foam around ships, wooden piles or wood generally.

In an American legends the sea gave birth to the land. The Indians living along the banks of the Mississippi say that a woman came from the heavens and leapt several times in the air, not knowing where to set down her foot. Then the turtle offered her its back, and she accepted it. Soon all the impurities of the sea gathered round the turtle and thus the land was formed. The Kalmuks have a similar legend: at first there was only the ocean, then the winds whipped its surface into waves whose foam solidified to form the continents.

One of the Greek traditions about Venus tells that she was born from the foam of the sea, just as was Lakshmi, the beloved of Siva, in Hindu mythology.

One day in Palembang a great mass of foam was seen floating on the water, and from this foam was born a girl of immense beauty. When Sang Superba was told of this he ordered the girl to be brought to him and named her Tundjang Buyeh ("Born of the Water").

When the tidal rise and fall is very small, the French say the sea is *en morte-eau* ("in dead water", i.e. neap-tide). In several other languages the idea of a neap-tide is expressed by the same image—*doodt waater, doodt strom* (Dutch), *agoas mortas* (Portuguese), *aqua morta* (Italian).

High tide is called in French *la vive eau* ("the living water"), an expression which also has its parallels in other languages.

Proverbs (2)

Tout flux a son reflux (French: Every tide has its ebb).

Na hooge vloeden diepe ebben (Dutch: "After high water comes low water").

Na de ebbe komt vloed, en de frienden met het goed (Dutch: After the ebb comes the flood, and friends bringing riches).

Lukka er liksom sjoen: stumdom felle of stendom flöder (Norwegian: Luck is like the sea, sometimes it rises, sometimes it falls).

The highest tides are followed by low water (German).

The higher flood has always the lower ebb (English).

Hoe hooger boom, hoe leeger val; na hooge vloeden, diepe ebben (Flemish: The higher the tree, the harder it falls; the highest tides give way to the lowest ebbs).

The English proverb "Time and tide wait for no man" has its exact counterpart in French *(Le temps et la marée n'attendent personne)* and German *(Zeit und Ebbe warten auf niemand)*. In Scotland they say: "Time and tide nae man bide."

The French proverb *"La marée n'attend personne"* ("The tide waits for nobody") implies that one must make use of opportunities. A 15th century version runs: *La mer n'attend pas le roi* ("The sea won't wait for the king").

The expression "to have the wind and the tide with you" means having the best conditions for success. By contrast "to have wind and tide against you" means to be in a bad way. "To go against wind and tide" is to pursue one's objectives despite all obstacles. There is a similar expression in Portuguese: *Ir contra vento e mare.*

In Upper Brittany they say: "He is going to be head on to the tide" to refer to a slow moving person who, like the ship which has the tide full against it, is in danger of having a hard time achieving his aims.

The French say of an empty bottle that it is *à marée basse* ("at low tide").

In Brittany they say to someone they fear is going to be late, *Tu vas manquer la marée* ("You'll miss the tide").

Beza warlec'h ar mare o pesketa ("going fishing when the tide is out") means doing something at an unsuitable time.

C'est quand le rocher est découvert qu'il faut pêcher ("Go fishing when the rock is above water") refers figuratively to people who do not work hard when times are good and thus face poverty when times are hard.

Tides

In classical times navigation was long confined to the Mediterranean where, as is common knowledge, there are hardly any perceptible tides. If the coasts of Greece had, like those of Gaul, been alternately covered and uncovered by the sea, it is probable that the Greeks would have had gods of the tides. But in fact this natural phenomenon was so little known to the Greeks that they were amazed and terror-stricken when the fleet of Alexander the Great was left high-and-dry in the Indian Ocean. When Julius Caesar's soldiers reached Brittany, they were almost equally surprised by the tides. In the days of Pausanias it is maintained that the sea of the Gauls was impossible to navigate because of the tides, reefs and monsters.

However, the philosophers and writers of classical times were aware of the phenomenon and had various tentative explanations for it.

Some of them are given by Pomponius Mela, amongst them the one advanced by Plato, who saw the universe as a kind of living, moving organism. "It is not yet known whether the universe attracts and repels the waters on all sides (assuming, as do certain scholars, that the world is an animal), or whether there are caves at the bottom of the sea which draw in and pour forth the waters by turns, or whether, indeed, the moon influences these extraordinary movements."

In one of his *Letters to the Indians* Apollonius claims that the advance and withdrawal of the sea is caused by under-sea winds which come from caves unterneath the sea or along its shores. The tide is produced by a movement similar to that of respiration.

Fontanelle writes that Chinese philosophers elaborated the following theory to explain the phenomenon of tides: a princess had a hundred children, fifty of whom lived on the coast, while the other fifty lived in the mountains. From these groups arose two great nations who are frequently at war with one another. When the coast-dwellers have the upper hand over the mountain people and push them inland, it is the tide coming in. When the coast dwellers are thrown back and flee from the mountains to the shore, it is the ebb-tide.

According to a Hindu myth a huge mountain was placed in the sea. Wasuki, King of the Serpents, bound it round with rope. Vishnu, changed into a turtle, lay down underneath Wasuki to hold him up. When the rope was pulled the mountain turned, and this continual motion stirs up the sea and causes tides.

According to a medieval belief which was still current in the days of Columbus, the monstrous back of the Kraken used to rise up from the depths of the sea at regular intervals, its blow-holes throwing up vast waterspouts and breathing in equally huge quantities of air. Having done this, the Kraken would dearly have liked to frolic on the surface, but an iron hand, the black hand of Satan, used to drag it back into the depths. From this double motion of the world's living lung came the tides.

A similar tradition is found in the Shetland Islands. Here people used to believe in an enormous monster living in a remote part of the sea, whose breathing caused the tides. An old man called John Georgeson maintained that, far out to sea at the edge of the world, there lived a monstrous sea-serpent who took six hours to breath in and another six to breath out, which for him at any rate was a satisfactory explanation for tidal flow.

The people of Northern Germany say that the Man in the Moon is a giant, who, at the turn of the tide, bends down, takes up water and throws it down to earth, thus causing the tide to come in. But at the time of the ebb he stands upright again and stops work, so that the waters recede.

To walkers on the shore the sound of the rising tide sometimes seems like rather monotonous music. According to the sailors of Upper Brittany, this is what the sea says:

You who look at me with such curious eyes,
I am brought here by the moon in the heavens,
The moon brings me back time after time,
Cries to me sometimes so loudly that my head aches.
    Grieving sea,
    Go on your way
    Take all and leave nothing behind.

In the same area it is said that if you put your ear to a trumpet shell you can hear the tide rolling in. The sound will last as long as the tide does.

In England children hold a seashell to their ears and listen with delight to what they think is the sound of the waves.

Several legends show the sea withdrawing or interrupting the regularity of its tides to give way to statues of saints, religious processions and heroes, sometimes even to save lives of people in danger.

At Ploumanac'h on the day of the Pardon of St. Kirek, the sea retires before his statue and chapel. At Loaven on St. Liboubane's Day the tide holds back for an hour for the convenience of pilgrims.

In days gone by on the Feast of Corpus Christi, when the Blessed Sacrament was carried in procession around Concarneau, the tide used to go out to make way for it, whenever high tide coincided with the route of the procession.

Certain historians believed that the Pamphylian Sea withdrew to allow the passage of Alexander the Great's army when he was marching against the Persians. Josephus accepts the story in order to confirm the Jews' beliefs that their ancestors had passed through the Red Sea in much the same way.

The phenomenon of tides is so remarkable that those who see it daily ascribe to it a considerable influence over people and things. This belief is just as natural as that which sees the stars as the arbiters of man's destiny, indeed it is founded on facts which are more directly experienced and apparently consistent, though not accurately observed.

On the coast of Brittany it was long thought that babies were generally born when the tide was coming in. However, in the Tréguier region they are believed to arrive at ebb-tide.

According to a Breton belief male children are conceived at the time of the rising tide, girls when the tide is receding.

Along the coast of Brittany invalids are thought to feel worse when the tide is coming in, to be calmer at slack water and to feel better when the tide is going out. In Upper Brittany an invalid's strength returns as the tide rises, he struggles at slack water and grows weaker at the ebb.

When the tide is in one must avoid making faces, for fear one's face might be permanently fixed in a grimace. The following legend from the Tréguier area makes this very point: everyone knows that the people of the coast tell the time by the movements of the sea. One day a lady, a stranger to those parts, was passing along the shore, walking quickly because she had a long journey in front of her. She saw a little plaice sunning itself in a clear stream. "Little plaice, is the tide coming in?" asked the lady. But instead of answering, the plaice began to mock the lady by repeating her words and making faces at her.

At that time the tide began coming in, and the stranger (who was none other than the Blessed Virgin Mary) said to the fish: "Little plaice with your mouth askew, another time you will be wiser." The little plaice's mouth stayed askew, and since then every plaice has been the same.

A similar belief relating to the wind is found along the Channel coast. Here they also say that if you look upwards when the tide begins to go out, you might be frozen in this attitude.

In Upper Brittany you can be sure to catch a bad cold if you cut your hair when the tide is coming in.

In classical times there was a belief, shared by scholars, that people died only at the ebb-tide. Aristotle said that no animal dies except at the ebb. This according to Pliny, was often observed in the Sea of the Gauls and proven in the case of human beings. Apollonius maintains that he observed the truth of the matter at Gades.

This belief outlasted the Middle Ages. Shakespeare refers to it in "Henry V" (Act II, Scene 3): "A' (= he, Falstaff) parted even just between twelve and one, even at the turning of the tide". In many parts of the world it is still believed that people only die when the tide starts to come in.

In Portugal it is said that deaths occur when the tide is going out, and the same view is widely held in America. Fenimore Cooper in *the Spy* refers to it in two places, of which the following is the more characteristic:

I thought that his time had come.

No, he will live till the tide goes out or until cock-crow.

This belief also exists in Cornwall and Northumberland.

The author of a certain *Traité des erreurs et préjugés* (Treatise on errors and ancient beliefs) writes that this popular belief was once shared by doctors in all the ports in France, England and Holland, adding: "In the previous century a commissioner of the Mercantile Marine who was also a member of the Paris Academy of Sciences asked the members of the Order of Charity who ran

44

a hospital in Brest to note the exact time when the sick died. According to the registers they kept for the years 1727, 1728 and the early months of 1729 the number of those who died while the tide was rising was greater by two than the number of those who died on the ebb. The same research was done at Rochefort, St Malo, Quimper and other places, with the same result".

Tides also have an observable influence on animals. When the tide is coming in, mad dogs feel it and are worse that at other times. They run to and fro on the shore, bite the shingle and rush head-down into the foam of the sea, a thing they never do at the ebb. (Brittany.)

In Upper Brittany, when the pupil of a cat's eye is very dilated, they say it is high tide. If the pupil is small and veiled, they say that the tide is fully out.

In Finistère they believe that the pupils of cats' eyes change color and increase in size when the tide begins to come in.

In Upper Brittany and the area around Boulogne people wait until low water before killing pigs, as the bacon is then better and more abundant. In Lower Brittany male pigs are slaughtered when the tide rises and sows when it falls. In some places along the Channel coast pigs are killed when the tide is coming in, in the belief that bacon put in the larder is like the sea: it swells but does not shrink. It is also said that such meat swells when cooking.

In the north-east of Scotland there are farmer's wives who put their eggs under broody hens when the tide is going out so that only hens will be hatched. If this is done when the tide is rising, roosters will result.

Housewives in Brittany believe that the best time for making butter is when the tide begins to come in.

Bretons also believe that eiderdowns and feather beds filled with the feathers of sea-birds swell when the tide rises. In Pliny's day there was a similar superstition: "The hides of salt-pasture cattle, even when detached from the carcase, retain a sympathy with the sea. Every time the tide goes out the hairs stand on end."

On the coast of Brittany people firmly believe that changes in the weather often coincide with the tides. In Upper Brittany it is said that rain often begins at high tide, and in Finistère they have the saying: "With the tide comes the rain."

It is almost generally believed that a storm breaks only when the tide rises, and can be made to blow over by the tide going out. A storm is believed to return with the tide if it started when the tide was rising, and sometimes this can go on for nine days. This number is applied by peasants in inland areas to summer storms, which they say last nine days.

45

It has long been observed along the shores of the North Sea, the Bay of Bengal and other coastal areas that storms break out almost always when the tide is coming in. Thus scientific observation confirms popular beliefs.

The inhabitants of the Ile de Batz have two interesting sayings: "When the tide is half way out the bad weather improves" and "At mid-tide the weather turns fair or foul."

Tide and wind interreact. In Upper Brittany, if the wind blows from the north-west when the tide sets in, the same wind will accompany the rising tide for the whole cycle.

On the Ile de Batz people say: "When high tide comes at midday there will be windy weather."

In Finistère they think that at high tide the stronger the winds the quicker the tide will go out. The slighter the wind, the quicker the tide will come in.

In Scotland, when the tide is higher than usual, people expect a storm. In such cases the fishermen of Pittulie say that the height of the tide is caused by a storm-wind blowing in from the sea.

In Spain it is thought that if a north-east breeze springs up when the tide comes in, the latter will be abnormally high. When the wind blows from the sea, it will be at its strongest at high tide.

To judge from a particular passage from Shakespeare an irregularity in the tides foretold great evils to come. Clarence, in *Henry IV, Part I* (Act IV, Scene 5), says these words:

> The river hath thrice flow'd, no ebb between;
> And the old folk, time's doting chronicles,
> Say it did so a little time before
> That our great grandsire, Edward, sick'd and died.

The event referred to is a historical fact and occurred on 12th October 1411.

In France there was a belief current in the 17th century that an ebb-tide occurred earlier than expected is a sign of a coming storm.

In Upper Brittany sailors still foretell the future from the mood of the sea as seen in their dreams.

If one dreams of the sea at a time when the tide is going out, it is a sign that a parent will die and be borne away by the sea. If, on the other hand, this dream occurs when the tide is coming in, one can be sure of having news of a parent making a sea-voyage. Girls like dreaming of the sea because it means that they will have news of friends.

The tide-race has various significant names. In Montevideo it is called the "sea-quake" and in the Baltic *Seabären* (sea-bears).

On the West Coast of Ireland, fiven fairly rare combinations of wind and tide, a tide-race is created. The fishermen call it the "wave of vengeance". They describe it in frightening terms and recount a legend of how it came about. A certain fishermen once killed a mermaid, despite her pleas for mercy. The next time he set sail a terrible storm got up, and despite his efforts to flee he was dorwned with all his crew. The same tide-race appeared whenever his descendants put to sea.

Once near Vancouver the tide went out in a strange way, uncovering a large stretch of shore. This lasted for four days, and the local Indian tribe, the Seshat, thought nothing of it. There was one man, Wispohahp, who foresaw that this ebb would be followed by an equally extreme high tide. Accordingly he went into the forest to gather materials out of which he made a tremendously strong cable. Near his village was a rock at whose base grew trees well known for their strength.   He tied his boat to them and then went on board with his wife, brothers, their wives and all their most precious possessions. Then they waited.

After four days the sea started to come in. Half-way up the shore it began to rush in with terrible speed. The Seshat ran for their boats, some asking Wispohahp if they could share the use of his cable. Fearing that it might break, he refused, and would not even allow them to put their wives in his boat. Soon they were caught in the rising waters, and while the far-sighted Wispohahp lay safely at anchor, they were swept out to sea by the irresistible force of the current. In the end the whole land was submerged, even Quossakt, a high mountain. When four days has passed the sea receded, so Wispohahp pulled on his cable. When the sea had returned to its normal level, Wispohahp found he was still near the site of his village.

Diodorus Siculus reports a similar legend, probably brought back from the shores of the Indian Ocean by Greek or Phoenician seafarers: "The Ichtyophagi say that one day the tide went out so far that it uncovered the green depths of the sea-bottom. Hardly had this discovery been made when the sea suddenly returned to its usual place."

Some extremely high tides have left a terrible impression in the memories of men. For example: "In the port of Pisco various nobles and persons of quality, perceiving one day that the sea had suddenly gone out to a great distance, leaving the whole sea-shore high and dry, ran out to the beach in great numbers, not suspecting the disaster which was about to befall. For soon afterwards they saw a great swelling of the sea, and the waves increased in size, no longer waves but mountains of water so high that they lost all hope of saving their lives. Expecting to be overwhelmed at any moment they threw themselves on their knees and called upon the power of Him whom alone the winds and the sea obey. Lo and behold, the sea rose from its normal course and split in two, leaving untouched the place where the unfortunate people were kneeling, poured to the right and the left of them twenty feet deep and laid waste the whole countryside."

The tidal bore

At the mouths of certain rivers such as the Seine, Gironde, Severn, Elbe, Weser, Hooghly, Amazon etc. the meeting of the incoming tide and the river water causes one or more high waves.

In English this is called the bore. In French it is called *mascaret* or more significantly, *barre*, the verb *barrer* summing up the way the wave grows, breaks, collapses on itself and sends foaming water hurling from one bank of the river to another.

The bore of the river Amazon is called *Prororoca* because of its roaring sound and is said to consist of two or three waves at a time.

On certain parts of the coast of Africa the natives think that the bore is the work of a particular and malevolent god, who needs to be appeared by sacrifices. When the natives set off to cross the dangerous bore in the Gulf of Guinea, the witch doctor stands on the shore and tries to calm the evil spirit of the bore by ritual gestures and prayers.

Spells and incantations were used against the bore of the Tsien-Tang River.

In the year 930 Prince Wu Shu ordered five hundred picked archers to discharge six arrows each into the tidal bore; then, having prayed to Wu Tsz-si, the tutelary god of the river, he put the key of the canal gate in an envelope and cast it into the water. In 1131 the Emperor Kan Tsung threw into it six massive iron dishes to placate the evil spirits of the river.

The bore of the Meghna, one of the mouths of the Ganges, is several miles in extent. This disturbance of the waters is probably the origin of the legend about the cannon of Barisal whose report is brought to the ears of the coast-dwellers by the evening wind.

Hindu legend ascribes a supernatural origin to the Ganges bore, just as it does to so many other phenomena. It is said that Bagharata, having taken the divine Ganga as his bride in the land of snows, seized her in his arms, mounted his chariot and with its wheels traced out the limits of the bed to occupied by the goddess. But when Ganga arrived at the sea-shore, she shrank back in terror at the sight of the enormous ocean. She fled away through a hundred channels, and ever since those days she comes and goes twice a day, first venturing down to the sea, then fleeing back towards the mountains.

Is Bernardin de St. Pierre's charming legend in *L'Arcadie* the result of a memory of a story heard long before or simply inspiration? It is a difficult question to answer. Here is his tale, whose ending has striking resemblances to that of the Hindu legend given above:

" Seine, daughter of Bacchus and nymph of Ceres, had followed the Goddess of Corn into the land of the Gauls in her search for her daughter Proserpine. When Ceres had ended her journey, Seine asked her for the gift of those meadows you see yonder. The goddess agreed and granted the daughter of Bacchus in addition the power of making wheat grow wherever she went. She left Seine upon the shore and gave her the nymph Héva as companion and attendant. Héva was to watch over her, lest she be taken away by some sea-god, as her daughter had been carried off by the god of the underworld. One day Seine was running over the sand looking for shells and uttering loud cries as the waves of the sea splashed her feet and sometimes came up to her knees. Suddenly Héva saw beneath the waves the white horses, flushed cheeks and blue robe of Neptune. This god had come from the Orkneys after a great earthquake and was cruising along the shore, testing the sea-bed with his trident to see whether it was still firm. When she caught sight of him Héva gave a great cry and warned Seine, who immediately fled towards the meadows. But the sea-god had seen the nymph of Ceres and, struck by her light-footed grace, urged his sea-horses up the shore after her. He had almost caught her when she called for the aid of her father Bacchus and her mistress Ceres. Both of them heard her prayers. As Neptune was reaching out to seize her, Seine's body was turned into water. Her veil and her green robe, blown before her by the wind,

52

became emerald-green water. She was changed into a river of the same color and still delights to wander through the places she once loved as a nymph. Even stranger, Neptune, despite her metamorphosis, has not ceased to be in love with her, as the river Alphaeus in Sicily is said to love the nymph Arethusa still. But though the sea-god still loves Seine, she retains her aversion for him. Twice each day he pursues her with great roars, and each time Seine flees to her meadows, running upstream, contrary to the usual way of rivers. She always keeps her green waters separated from the blue waters of Neptune".

Waves

In Brittany they use the graceful and accurate image *mer fleurie* (flowery sea) to describe the sea when its waves break in foam without becoming rough. The unknown author of the *Life of St. Condède* depicts the waves moving with a great roar and raising their crests plumed with foam like great trees with thick foliage. The common people have preserved this image still and say that the wave *fleurit* (blossoms) when its crest is crowned with foam.

Poets have always used color-terms to describe waves. Homer calls them "whitening" when in the open sea they seem to have great depth.

English sailors (Russel: *Sailors' Language*) use the term "a green sea" for masses of water which move towards a ship without breaking against it. The author of a history of Sumatra relates that some of the people of that country think that sea-water is by its very nature continually in motion. A man who observed its unceasing restlessness took a vaseful to his own country and poured it into a lake, confident that it would continue the same surging motion there.

Poets ascribe the same will to motion to the waves themselves, depicting them as rational beings or as animals. In Homer the waves grow angry, roll their irritated crests and break with a roar. Moschus (*Idylls*, Book V) speaks of "mutinous waves". The Greek poets are full of similar images, and the tradition is continued by the Latin ones. Propertius speaks of "threatening waves", others compared them to warriors charging or to sailors boarding an enemy ship.

In the *Iliad*, Chapter XVI, Neptune, trident in hand, leads the waves in an attack on the Greek ramparts. The same image occurs several times in the *kalevala:* Wainamoinen's ship resists the battering of the great waves, old, dauntless Wainamoinen steers it with a sure hand, despite the onslaught of the boiling waves. The Swedish poet Tegner, who draws his inspiration largely from folk-poetry and its images, has waves "rushing as if to board the half-swamped ship".

Just as warrior-like passions have been ascribed to waves, poets have endowed the sea with the impulsiveness of great heroes. Homer, in Chapter VI of the *Iliad* compares the Greeks going off to war to great waves which rear up near the shore raised by the powerful breath of Zephyrus. Out at sea they force each other onwards, then, quaking, break against the shore or its headlands, their backs bristling with foam. The same image occurs in a Tahitian war-song: "Hurl yourselves, we say to warriors, hurl yourselves like the waves; break over your enemies like the foam of the sea..."

Several mythologies liken waves to gods. In that of the Greeks the names of certain sea-nymphs seem to contain an allusion to the waves they are named after: Cynothoë (Swift Wave), Speio (The swift one), Dynamene (The Mighty), Cynodoce (She Who Receives the Wave), Hippothoë (Swift Mare) and so on. As will be seen later, in Lower Brittany the waves have names like Hippothoë's.

In Scandinavian mythology the waves are wholly divine, daughters of Oegir and Ran. The Edda gives the names of the nine waves to whom they give birth. Drobna, the foaming water, is also one of the daughters of Gimer and Ran. The Estonians have a Lady of the Water who is in fact a goddess of the waves.

In the Kurile Islands the people call the waves *Kamui* (god), and when crossing the sea they throw overboard little carved figures to ensure a safe passage.

In Polynesia the god of the waves inhabits rocks. In the Hervey Islands the God Tikoruna is the storm-wave.

In Maori folklore heroes do battle with the waves. A huge wave swept in from the sea to kill Tawaki, but his ancestor Kaiaia (the kite) appeared and called, "Ke Ke Ke!" Tawaki woke up, seized a club and fought off the wave.

Japanese traditions tell that Isanaghi and Isanami turned the droplets of spray which fly up from the crests of waves into tutelary spirits.

When the sea gets up and the waves have white crests, people in many countries describe it by using a term similar to the French *moutonner* (to curl or froth white), from the word *mouton* (sheep). Sometimes they use expressions like "There are sheep in the meadow" for the same purpose. This is a natural image favored by peoples separated from each other by long distances. It is based on the same analogy as that between cloud formation and a fleece or sheep-fold.

The same idea is contained in the Scottish expression "the sheep afore the dog", denoting the heavy swell which precedes the storm.

In classical times the same image was used: the "flocks of Proteus" were in fact white-crested waves stirred up by the wind and the sea, suggesting to the mind the image of flocks of sheep.

The waves and the swell, because their sound resembles howling, suggest the dog image. Thus in Scotland they say "the dog afore his maister" to denote the heavy swell which comes before the storm. By contrast the swell that remains after the storm has abated is called "the dog ahin his maister". In Brittany a little wave which follows a larger one in known as "the dog who follows his master" in much the same way.

Millié, in a note to bis translation of the *Lusiad*, writes that Portuguese navigators named a newly discovered land *Sierra Leoa* (Lion Mountain, now Sierra Leone) because the sound of the waves breaking on the shore was like the distant roaring of a lion.

In many countries gods were thought to preside over the waves. Amongst the Greeks and Latins Neptune was the one who raised up the waves or calmed them. Venus Salacia was originally only the goddess of the movement of the waves. Sometimes they were at the call of the wind-gods.

The ancient Scandinavians, who believed the waves to be the daughter of the sea-goddess Rana, also thought that the movement of the sea was caused by gods or spirits. According to Thorpe they believed it was Thor who hurled roaring waves against cliffs and formed whirlpools in rocky places. The merciless waves raised by the Trolls in the *Saga of Frithiof* caused shipwreck. Ecke was the God of the North, the tides and the waves (Grimm). In Finnish mythology Aallotar, daughter of the waves, governs them. The *Kalevala* also mentions Ahto, King of the Blue Waves.

In Hawaii gods command the winds and the waves. At Nuka-Hiva the whistling of the storm-wind and the noise of the waves were seen as signs of the god's displeasure. In a Norwegian legend the sea became rough when a certain giant beat the shore with his foot.

In Portugal the movement of the sea is explained as punishment from God. St. Peter holds two keys, it is said, one of them for Heaven, the other for the sea. The first is gold, the second black. At the creation of the world God condemned all water, including the water of the sea, to be always in motion. Despite its ceaseless movement the sea cannot escape from its bed, thanks to the power of St. Peter's key.

On the coast of Upper Brittany sailors believe that the waves are produced by the wind. They also believe that they can be caused by dew.

Seafarers use the appearance of the waves, their color and above all their sound to foretell the future and forecast the weather.

According to Scandinavian folklore the sound of the waves on a certain part of the shore is the murmuring of a king and queen of ancient times, who lie buried in nearby mounds. The groans of the sea near Elsinore foretell death.

The sound of Nasjoir, the death-wave of Icelandic tradition, is like the groaning of a man in agony.

On the coast of Cork, when the waves make an unusual sound, people say it is a sign of the death of a great man.

A story well-known in Saint-Jean-de-Luz gives a pleasant if impractical suggestion for calming the waters. One day two women were walking by the sea. One of them, seeing the ocean for the first time and amazed by the fury of the waves, said to her friend, "Is the sea married?" "No," was the reply. "Ah! If only the sea were married, it wouldn't be such a terrifying sight." The same story is told on the coast of Asturias.

In many countries sailors ascribe certain qualities and sometimes certain supernatural powers to a succession of waves, three, nine or ten. This belief is based partly on over-generalised observations which seemed to point to a periodic regularity in the movements of the sea. There is also a connection here with ancient popular beliefs about fatidical or magic numbers.

In Brittany they say that every third wave is more powerful than the others. When the tide rises, the third wave washes over the sand which the others have merely wetted. It is also the one that makes the most noise when breaking on the shore. On the coast of Finistère it is widely believed that the third wave is the strongest, or at least the most feared, and people have a saying: "We have weathered the first two waves, beware of the third!"

Sailors think that after three bad waves the sea becomes calmer.

In Scotland they believe that in a storm there are three heavy waves, the third being weaker and less dangerous. This succession is called a "rote of waves".

In the Shetland Islands there is a tradition that before the introduction of the compass experienced fishermen found their way back to port in the thickest fog by looking at the way the waves moved and judging the direction of the land from this. But this skill seems to have been lost by later generations of fishermen, probably because they no longer needed it.

Icelandic fishermen say that there are three big waves called *olag*, which follow one another in succession. No boat should be launched until immediately after the third. If a boat is wrecked during this operation, they say, a great calm will come over the sea, called *dautklag* (death calm), and while it lasts the other boats are safe.

In the Shetland Islands, according to the Folklore Journal, in fairly recent times peoples credited the third wave with even greater powers: they believed toothache could be cured by sea-water drawn from the crest of the third wave.

The water on the far side of the third wave, that is, the wavelet that washes around one's feet on the shore, was seen as possessing great power and was used to cast spells, ward off evil or wreak vengeance. Only initiates could use it without danger to themselves, because it was a two-edged weapon. The term "third-die", though it seems to imply death, in fact means no more than "third wave".

In certain legends about the third waves witches assume the form of waves to sink the ships of those they hate or wish to be revenged on. In that case the danger to the ship can only be averted by striking the wave with a sword.

According to a folk-tale from the Basque region of Spain, *The Three Waves*, one night as a cabin boy was lying on deck apparently asleep, he saw two women come down from the sky. They took the ship through the air to an orchard of olive strees, went away for a time, then returned and took the ship back to the place from which they had brought it. Then one of the women told the other that all on board the ship would die, as she would raise up three huge waves out the calm sea, the first of milk, the second of tears and the third of blood. "There is only one way of escaping this fate", said the older woman to the younger "and that is to throw a harpoon into the third wave, for this wave, the wave of blood, will be me. I shall be hidden beneath the water, and the blow which strikes this wave will pierce my heart". When the ship was out at sea the cabin-boy told the captain the whole story. The latter ordered one of his men to throw a harpoon into the third wave. He did so, and a loud groan was heard. The wave split in two before the stem of the ship and covered the shore with bloody foam. That day the ship had a good catch, as the spell was broken. But when he returned home the captain found his wife ill in bed, and soon afterwards she died, calling down curses on her husband and his nephew, the harpooner. She was the witch who had kept the boat under a spell.

This tale of the three magic waves is also known in the North. In Schleswig-Holstein they have a story in which three men from North Friesland were away at sea in the same boat. In the meantime their wives dabbled in witchcraft. Not trusting their husbands, the women followed them in different forms, discovered their husbands infidelities and decided to have their revenge by sinking the boat. As they were standing on the deck making their plans, thinking everyone had gone ashore, a cabin-boy heard all they said, including the words, "All will go well, provided no pure soul fights us off with an unblooded sword". The cabin-boy got hold of a new sword, and in the storm that had got up walked along the deck on the windward side. Soon he saw three waves approaching the ship, as high as towers and as white as snow. He thrust at them with his sword. At that very instant the waves grew calm, and the sword was stained with blood. When the ship landed at Hamburg the captain and his two crewmen learned that their wives had suddenly been taken ill on the night when the three waves had appeared. The other variant of this story comes from Oldenburg. As in the Basque version, the master discovered the secret while seeming to be asleep. Warned in advance, the sailors struck the first wave with an ax, and the deck was covered in blood. They struck the second with a saw, with the same result. They struck the third with a double-headed ax and once again the deck was covered in blood. They completed their voyage safely, and when they returned to their homes, they found the captain's wife and her two sisters maimed and mutilated.

According to Celtic tradition the ninth wave is bigger than the others and surges further up the shore. It also had certain powers, traces of which can be found in certain ancient Celtic works of literature. When the Tuatha De Danann were faced with a sudden invasion by the Milesians (one of the legendary peoples of ancient Ireland) they reached an agreement with the invaders by which the latter were to re-embark and move out to the sea "to a distance of nine waves". Then, if the invaders succeeded in landing by force, the Tuatha De Danann would surrender the port to them. The Milesians agreed, but when they had passed the distance of nine waves their enemies used magic spells to raise a tempest against them, scattering the whole fleet like chaff.

At Colunga on the coast of Asturias the ninth wave is reputed to be stronger than the others. It is known as *la zorea.*

Allatius tells us that in the 17th century the way to avoid the fatal impact of the ninth wave was to make the sign of the cross while murmuring certain special prayers. Sea-captains saw the ninth wave as the only one which could harm their ships, so that they repeated their prayers every ninth wave.

The open sea

The term "open sea", that is, that part of the sea which lies at a certain distance from the shore and is not enclosed or bounded by land, conveys the impression of space. An equivalent term is "the high seas", corresponding to the Latin *in altum*.

Folk traditions and mythologies often tell of gods, genii or heroes who have the power to walk on the surface of the sea or indeed sleep on it, gently rocked by the waves.

Neptune roved the waves in a chariot drawn by sea-horses. Amphitrite and other sea-gods did the same. The Gospels say that Jesus walked on the waters of Lake Tiberias and that he invited St. Peter to come to him in the same way. Odin, mounted on his horse Sleipnir, rode over the sea as well as the land. In Tahiti, Hiro, the sea-god, was a great traveler who roved the sea in all directions, sometimes on the surface and sometimes in the depths. Certain giants of the Middle Ages, like Gargantua, were so huge that they could cross the sea on foot.

One of Vishnu's commonest names is Narayana, who has his home in the waters. He is portrayed as sleeping peacefully on the surface of the sea.

Certain Scandinavian heroes or demigods were able, like the gods themselves, to walk on the waters, which seemed like solid land under their feet. It is said that Jode of Uppsala could be seen galloping on the waters with his black horses. The Cliff-King also passed over them in his chariot drawn by four black horses. The goddess Holda did the same. In Finnish mythology Vainamoinen crossed the sea on his horse which was as light as a feather, without the water wetting his hooves and without touching its surface.

According to Hawaian legend a giant who was the brother of a hero of those parts passed from island to island by walking on the sea. Russian traditions say that Czar Morskoi, King of the Sea, used the sea as a highway.

Eskimo folklore tells of demons called Tornit who pass over the sea during storms without needing a boat.

When Christianity had destroyed the ancient pagan religions, the power of walking on the waters, formerly a feature of the dethroned gods, was transferred to the saints, who were now heirs of their divine attributes and who, in any case, were only imitating their Master. At one time it was even believed that the saints, because of their holiness, could walk over the water without sinking into it at all.

Père Fournier gives numerous examples: "During the persecution of Decius St. Tyrsus was cast into the sea for the sake of the faith and walked on it as if on land. When St. Charitina the Virgin was thrown into the sea with a large stone tied round her neck, the rope broke, the stone sank to the bottom, and the saint walked on the waters as if on *terra firma*, returning to the judge who had condemned her to death. Saints Nazaire and Celsus, having been thrown into the sea, returned from it by the power of God. When St. Pantaleon was cast into the sea with a stone round his neck, the stone floated like wood, and the saint came back to the shore walking on the waters."

In the *Life of St. Ignatius Loyola* the captain of the Venetian vessel in which the founder of the Company of Jesus had embarked for the Holy Land is reported to have said to him: "Why are you making this crossing on board my ship? A saint has no need of such ordinary devices. He walks on the waters like Christ."

One day when Scothinus was travelling in way over the Irish Sea he met his brother St. Banas, who was passing on a ship. The latter, who did not possess the same magic powers, seems to have become very jealous of Scothinus and asked querulously what he was walking upon. Scothinus replied that he was walking over a beautiful plain. As St. Banas rejected this with scorn, Scothinus stopped and picked a handful of beautiful flowers. In reply St. Banas also stopped, plunged his hand into the sea and came up with a handful of fishes. St. Aidan was also fond of riding over the sea and had a horse specially trained for this purpose.

Other saints had the power of moving over water using their cloaks, like Faust. St. Hyacinth and St. Francis de Paul did the same. These pious legends arise from the medieval belief that saints bodies weighed less than those of ordinary men.

The Devil and witches are also credited, if less frequently with the power of walking on the sea.

There are legends that link the origin of certain patches on the surface of the sea and certain visible currents with the passing of gods and saints over the water. Near St. Malo the term *sentes de la Vierge* (paths of the Virgin) is used to denote streaks lighter in color than the rest of the sea. They are said to foretell good weather. According to legend they mark the presence of the Virgin descending over the sea to calm it.

In a bay in Brittany, when the weather is calm and the tide is in, a kind of furrow is seen, the "furrow of St. Germain". Once when a pilgrimage was being made to the chapel which bore his name, his statue happened to be at Plévenon, on the other side of the bay. However, the weather was so bad that no boat could cross over to fetch it. To avoid disappointing the pilgrims, the saint's statue crossed the bay of its own volition, leaving the white furrow in the sea as it passed. In Finland people call the white streaks which appear on the surface of the sea after a storm "the path of Vainamoinen" or more precisely "the wake of Vainamoinen's ship". Vainamoinen was supreme god of the Finns.

Currents

In French strong currents are called *courants de foudre* (lightning currents), *courants d'enfer* (hell-currents) and *courants du diable* (the Devil's currents).

Certain currents famous for their force and strength have individual names. In the Aegadian Archipelago dangerous currents and sudden changes in the level of the sea are known to the natives as "marubia" or "drunken sea".

Off Storma in the Pentland Firth roars the redoubtable Swelkie whirlpool, said by the Edda to be the ceaseless mill which grinds the salt of the sea. The same tradition applies to the Maelstrom produced by the magic mill in the legend already described.

This, the most famous of all the whirlpools is to be found of the coast of Norway. Its name means literally "grinding current". This refers to the way it revolves, seeming to engulf floating objects just as a mill takes in grain, and also to its origins as described in the legend. Edgar Allan Poe wrote a vivid description of it in his *Descent into the Maelstrom.*

Once it was thought that the maelstrom travelled about the world. Oläus Magnus described it as a beast with a lamprey-like mouth which it used to swallow ships. Cannons had no effect on it, though trumpets could be used to scare it off.

The Strait of Naruto is feared by Japanese sailors, who see it as similar to the Maelstrom.

According to *Les Relations des Jésuites de la Nouvelle France*, 1634, Chapter XIII, "some of the natives believe that there are waterfalls in the sea, wherein many ships are lost."

As currents are an important factor in navigation, proverbs about them are to be found in abundance.

Secundo aestu procedere (from Erasmus: To have the current in one's favor).

Lé cattivo navegâ contra a corrente (from Genoa: It is unwise to sail against the current).

No bisogna andar contra la corente (from Venice, as above).

Ne'er strive against the stream (from Scotland).

Tegen stroom is kwadd zwemmen (from Holland: It is difficult to swim against the current).

The veel is kwadd genoeg, ziij dat wat gij geniet; een schip vaart veiligst door een neet te sterken vliet (from Holland: Be glad of little things, avoid extremes: the ship sails safest in a gentle current).

The sea-bed

From earliest times there are allusions to the depth of the sea. It was seen as the epitome of depth. Thus it is written in the Book of Job: "Have you journeyed all the way to the sources of the sea, or walked where the abyss is deepest? An Indian proverb holds that "only the sea knows the depth of the sea".

The widespread belief that the sea was bottomless, or at least deeper than any other known thing, gave rise to the custom whereby people threw into it things they wished to be rid of for ever. To show that one wished to renounce something for ever or that a judgement was to be consigned to perpetual oblivion, the objects which represented it were cast into the sea. Thus it was that when Alcibiades returned to Athens the Athenians hurled into the sea the stones on which his banishment had been recorded.

Polycrates, tyrant of Samos, threw a precious ring into the sea as a kind of sacrifice. Legend has it that it came back to him in the stomach of a fish. There is a story that St. Gerbold, bishop of Bayeux, expelled from his see by the people of the town, cast his ring into the waters, declaring that he would not return until it had been found. Some years later he returned to his see, his ring having been recovered from a fish which had swallowed it.

In the Marquesas Islands, when the tribe which had eaten an enemy wished to make peace with his tribe, the victim's head was solemnly taken to the shore wrapped in a cloth and tied to a heavy stone. The, a canoe manned by Kanakas bearing palm-leaves sank it in the deepest part of the bay, there to remain, both head and vendetta buried for ever.

Popular tales of a widespread type tells of a princess casting golden keys into the sea, saying that she will not agree to marry until they have been found. The hero of the story usually succeeds in rescuing the keys with the aid of the King of the Fishes or one of the spirits of the deep. In a story told on the coast of Africa the king promises a grass-cutter to give him a wife if he can bring back a cymbal which the king has lost in the sea. The hero manages to do this with the help of an alligator. A parallel legend is told in Samoa.

The sea with its vast, deep waters has always seemed mysterious to ordinary people. Things glimpsed through clear sea-water or partly uncovered by the tide gave rise to the general notion that the sea-bottom was another world in itself, peopled like ours by beings that were good or bad, kind or cruel.

They lived in sea-dwellings: though the water could not reach them, through walls as clear as glass they could see shoals of fishes swimming past. Their ornaments were brightly-colored plants such as those sometimes cast up by the sea, mother-of-pearl glowing all the colors of the rainbow and many-hued seashells.

In Greek mythology Poseidon lived beneath the sea. The Iliad describes him as having a magnificent palace beneath the waters of the Aegean.

Great Triton was said to live in a golden palace under the sea. Like many other sea-gods the Nereïds lived there also, in caves or on the sea-bottom. According to Scandinavian folklore Oegir and his wife Ran lived in the sea; Ran put out blue cushions on the sand of the sea-bottom to welcome shipwrecked mariners. In Cochin China the King of the Underworld or the Spirits of the Waters bring back from the depths of the sea those who have been drowned and not been given proper burial. They set them to hard labor.

Ju-ru-win, the evil spirit of the sea, has several under-sea residences. With him live his wife and children who help him to eat the corpses of drowned men. Russian folklore tells of Czar Morskoi, King of the Waters and the Sea, who resides in the sea depths.

Eskimo folklore tells of Atalits, evil spirits who dwell on the sea-bed and lure down drowning men.

The Kaffirs believe that there are spirits living beneath the waves with their flocks and huts. The Zulus, too, believe that there are semi-humans living underneath the sea.

For the ancient Japanese the sea was the dwelling place of the *Kami*, or sea-spirits. According to the Kalevala a tiny man from the depths of the sea, the hero of the waves, comes up from the sea-bed no more than an inch high and then grows into a giant.

The Swedes have a legend which says that there are mermaids in the sea with houses, domestic animals and cattle, the latter known as *brand' cattle*. One tale describes the palace of the Lady of the Boundless Sea at the bottom of the sea as being adorned with pearls and precious stones. In the Shetland Islands they tell of the mermaids' palace of pearls and coral on the sea-bottom amongst the fish.

The Irish hero Maelduin once sailed over a sea so clear that its waters were like a light haze. In the depths could be seen fine houses set in woodlands.

Certain fairies were also said to live at the bottom of the sea. One day, when a sailor cast anchor it struck the back of a fairy who promptly threw it back to the top of the mast. When they came to let down the anchor a second time a sea-fairy advised them in future to shout "Sea-fairies, are you there?", and they had no further difficulty.

In a story called *Le fond de la mer* (The Bottom of the Sea) we are told that one day near Ushant, the sounding-lead brought up a valuable coin, which was given to a sailor, Pierre Capucin, a man not outstanding at his trade. The coin spoke to him and told him that there were many others at the bottom of the sea. Then it took a different shape to tempt him, the last being that of a pretty brunette who let him stroke her hair. Her hair grew longer and longer until it touched the sea fifty fathoms away from where they were sitting. At last he allowed himself to be persuaded to descend into the depths of the sea, where he saw the sea-bottom covered with diamonds. The woman showed him her magnificent palace where sausages grew from coconut trees, and told him that everything would be his if he would agree to accept her as his mother. He refused, and the whole delightful scene disappeared.

On the coast of Northern Brittany people believe that dragons live at the bottom of the sea in places where there are sunken ships with treasure in their holds, and stand guard over them.

In the Book of Job Leviathan makes the water at the bottom of the sea boil. A gigantic worm lives on the sea-bed, biting its own tail and encircling the whole world. The sea is said to be the dwelling place of the Serpent of Mitgard. John of Brompton tells two legends about the stormy nature of the Bay of Satalia; according to one the head of a huge serpent rests on the bottom, and when it raises its head it stirs up a terrible storm.

We have already seen above that the sea in general is sometimes called "the sailors' cemetery" and *le caveau de Dieu* (God's burial vault). These terms apply even more closely to the sea-bed. Many nations consider it as holy as consecrated ground. In the Tréguier area it is considered a hallowed place, and sailors who lie there are just as properly buried as those who lie in a churchyard. The same belief is to be found in Italy. In the middle of a storm Chateaubriand heard sailors praying for mariners *sepolti in questo sacro mare* (buried in this holy sea).

As a large number of people die by drowning at sea, coastal dwellers long believed that the sea held as many dead as the land. Indeed Breton sailors maintain that on Judgement Day the sea will yield up one more dead than the land.

In Scandinavian folklore there are legends about sea-bishops and about churches which rise up out of the waves. Here the bodies of those who have perished at sea lie until the Day of Judgement, enjoying a rest as peaceful as those buried in hallowed ground. One legend tells of a fisherman coming across a churchlike building in the sea, as firm as if it had been built on a rock. A flight of steps led to the church door. The fisherman moored his boat to the top step and went into the church, where in the quiet half-light he could seee the bodies of those who had been shipwrecked, some dressed in the fisherman's clothes they had been wearing when they met their end...

When the fisherman recognised the bodies of some of his friends, he was afraid and hurried out. He was just time, for the church was sinking, and the step to which he had moored his boat was already under water. He cut the rope and the instant he climbed into his boat the church disappeared beneath the sea.

If the sea is a cemetery, for certain people it is also a paradise. The Japanese believe in a paradise beneathe the waves. The Greenlanders locate their heaven under the sea: it is always summer, and there is food in abundance. Seals can be caught without any difficulty, in fact they jump into cauldrons which are always on the boil.

In a Swedish tale called *Princess Singorra* a king promised his son to a sea-goddess, but did not keep his word. One day the young prince was playing with other children on the shore when suddenly a snow-whit hand with golden rings on each finger came up out of the sea and snatched him away into the blue waves.

The young prince was borne across the sea to the realm of the sea-goddess, where he lived in her golden, bejewelled palace beneath the waters.

According to an Irish legend a mermaid who lived in the sea carried off Maurice, a musician. Off the coast of Kerry on calm nights sailors hear the sound of music coming up from the sea-bed, and those with sharp ears say they can make out the voice of Maurice and the sound of his bagpipes.

The folklore of many lands tells of cities buried under the sea, their church bells still to be heard. There are other bells too. On the coast around Tréguier sailors and fishermen often hear bells beneath the waves. Off the Sept-Iles can be heard the bell of Port-Blanc. Long ago it was carried off by English pirates but it slipped into the sea to escape from their hands.

An old folk tale from Hereford says that the bell from Kentsam Church was the largest bell ever made. Founded at the same time as Great Tom of York, Great Tom of Lincoln and Great Tom of Christchurch, all four were loaded onto the same ship and all except the great bell of Kentsam were put ashore safely. When it came to the latter's turn, the unloading was more difficult, and in the middle of it the sea-captain grew angry and began to curse and swear. Instantly the great bell burst its ropes and fell to the bottom of the sea. The work of raising it from the sea-bed was on the point of succeeding when the captain said:

"Despite all the devils in Hell
We have landed the Kentsam bell."

At that moment the ropes snapped again, the bell fell onto the sloping sea-bottom with a deafening peal and bounded away into the depths. It has never been seen since, but listeners on the shore have often heard it tolling on the sea-bed.

Long afterwards the twelve parish churches of Jersey each had a fine set of bells, but during a long civil war the States of Jersey decide to sell them all to pay their soldiers. So the bells were collected and sent to France. However, during the sea-crossing the vessel carrying them sank and all were lost, as if to demonstrate the anger of God at such a terrible sacrilege. Since then, during storms the bells have been heard ringing beneath the sea. To this day the fishermen of St. Ouen, before setting sail, always go down to the water and listen for the sound of bells borne on the wind. If they hear it, nothing in the world will persuade them to venture out.

Popular traditions often tell of gods, heroes or ordinary mortals who go down to the depths of the sea, sometimes to seek refuge, sometimes for other reasons. Here is a tale which proves how widespread was the belief that men could live under the sea. At the beginning of the 18th century a strange man-like creature climbed out of the sea and came aboard the merchant ship

Hirondelle, commanded by Captain Baker, and asked in Dutch for a pipe of tobacco. He was covered in scales and had fin-like hands. When asked who he was, he replied that he was Dutch, had embarked on a vessel at the age of eight, had gone down with all hands when the ship was wrecked and had lived in the sea ever since without any idea of how he had managed it.

An Indian legend tells that King Suran wanted to go to the sea-bed to find out what was in it. He had a glass box made, with a door which opened and closed. The King entered the box, which sank down onto the sea-bed. There the King saw vast treasures and came to a country whose inhabitants were amazed to learn that there was another world apart from their own. He married Sea-Moon, daughter of the king of that country. But as Suran grew homesick for the land, he went to the king, who gave him a sea-stallion. The prince mounted the horse, which bore him out of the sea and up into the sky. His Vizier caught sight of him and quickly took a fine mare down to the beach. The sea-stallion made straight for her, so that Suran was able to slip off his back onto the land. Then the sea-stallion returned to the waves.

Of the tales of men living under the sea, the commonest are those in which the men of the sea, enamoured of the daughters of the land, take them down to live in their palaces in the deep. Just as common are those in which mermaids or sirens take men down into the sea and marry them with their consent or without, and will only allow them to return to land under certain conditions.

An old merman, hearing a maiden boast of her beauty and compare it with that of a mermaid, carried her off to his palace of seashells and coral in the depths of the sea. There his son fell in love with her and married her by deceit. When she became bored with her life beneath the sea, her husband allowed her to return home for a time, warning her never to permit anyone to kiss her. She disobeyed her husband, forgetting him until one day he came to take her back with him to their home beneath the waves.

One day a poor girl of the diocese of Aarhus was gathering sand on the shore when she saw a merman emerge from the waves. His beard was greener than the sea and he was pleasant-looking. He told her that if she followed him he would give her as much money as she wanted. He took her by the hand and led her into the depths of the sea, where in due course she had six children. When she had been living there for a long time and had almost forgotten her Christian faith, one Sunday morning she heard the church-bells ringing and longed to go to church. The merman, seeing her weeping, asked the reason for her tears and allowed her to go to church, but warned her not to forget their children. In the middle of the sermon she heard the merman calling her from outside the church, but she decided to stay and hear the sermon through to the end. When it was finished he called her a second time, then a third, but in vain. At last he left, weeping bitterly, and went back to the sea. Thereafter she lived with her parents, leaving the merman to care for their children. His groans are often heard coming from the sea-bed.

The shore

Although sailors often speak deprecatingly of the land, it plays a very important part in their lives, and a wealth of superstitions and beliefs are attached to it.

The proximity of land was thought to influence the health of seafarers weakened by a long sea-voyage. Those who suffered from scurvy rallied at the prospect of the fresh food and greenstuffs which would restore their health.

In the 17th century people thought that dying sailors waited for landfall before finally giving up the ghost.

The old saying *terram video* (I spy land; in other words: I shall soon be out of danger) expressed the pleasure all felt at seeing land once again.

Certain kind of birds and fish were seen by sailors with great relief, as they were a sign that land was near. A certain kind of wasp follows a ship in great numbers until land is close by, then leaves the ship and flies off towards the shore.

Seafarers have often noticed that penguins never venture out into deep water, so when one appeared they could steer towards it, confident that land was not far off.

Sometimes the long-awaited sight of land was celebrated with great joy. Tavernier writes: "When we caught sight of the coast of Holland all the sailors of our fleet, which had taken part in the siege of Manilla, showed their happiness at seeing the coast of their own country once again by putting a large number of lighted candles of all sizes round the poop and bows of the vessel, where the wind could not blow them out." Near the island of Kassami the Turks expressed their joy at having escaped the perils of the sea by firing cannon and lighting up the ship. The sailors asked the passengers for money, which they then threw, box and all, into the sea.

Though the shore is often longed for, it is also feared, because it brings with it many more dangers than the open sea. Navigation demands constant vigilance, captains must watch out for currents, rocks and dangerous winds. To be shipwrecked near the shore is more tragic than on the open sea, as the ship is often smashed to pieces and its crew beyond rescue. Thus sailors use expressions like "on the rocks", "on one's beam-ends" to mean disaster generally.

Before the introduction of the compass mariners almost always sailed within sight of land and maintained that this was the most pleasant way to sail, just as on land the most enjoyable walk was one within sight of the sea.

The ceaseless noise of the sea is the origin of the Latin saying *Littori loqueris* (literally "you are speaking on the shore", which means "you are wasting your time").

From remote antiquity fires or lights have been lit on coasts to guide ships through the night. In many languages they bear the name of the lighthouse built on the island of Pharos at the entrance to the port of Alexandria. However, lighthouses do not figure much in folklore.

In classical times each shore had its guardian deities. People prayed to them when setting sail and offered sacrifices in thanksgiving when they had returned. Pausanias mentions a number of temples dedicated to sea-gods. They were generally sited on headlands, so that they could be seen by mariners from a long way off.

In the days of Diodorus Siculus sailors still venerated a spot near Byzantium which the Argonauts had dedicated to the gods by setting up altars there. When Christianity replaced paganism chapels and churches took the place of these high temples, many of them were dedicated to the Virgin Mary under names such us Our Lady of Grace, Our Lady of Succor. Others were dedicated to St. Savior (which seems like the epithet of a pagan god personified) or to local saints.

Chapels were built as a result of vows made when in danger from the sea. It is said that at the height of a great storm which raged in the middle of the night a sea-captain vowed to build a chapel to the Virgin on the first piece of ground he saw, if only he and his crew could land safe and sound. The moment he made his vow he saw a bright gleam (in French *clarté)* in the distance, made towards it and landed safely a few hours later. In fulfillment of his vow he built the beautiful chapel known as Notre Dame de la Clarté above the harbor of Ploumanac'h in Brittany.

Devotion to the saints of the shore lived on in some Protestant countries even after the Reformation. Probably something similar pre-dates Christianity. Walter Scott writes of a curious example: in the Shetland Islands the Church of St. Ringan used to preserve a few offerings made in earlier times. The simple fishermen of Dunrossness had a custom whose origin they had long forgotten, one which their minister tried in vain to suppress. When their boats were in great peril they used to vow to give an "awmous" or offering to St. Ringan. Once danger was past they never failed to keep their vow by going alone and unobserved to the ancient church. There they took off their shoes and stockings at the entrance to the churchyard and walked three times round the ruins from East to West and back.

At the end of the third day, to fulfill their vow they used to throw their offering, usually a small coin, through the broken tracery of a ruined window in a side wall. When they went away they took care not to look behind them until they had left the hallowed ground, for it was believed that the saint held the offering in his withered hand and showed his ghastly skull at the window.

Cliffs

At the seaside the waves collapse at the foot of natural obstacles which prevent their penetrating inland. Often these are high rocky cliffs which form a sort of wall with headlands as bastions. Sometimes there is a bay between two rocky points jutting out to sea, the land being protected not by solid stone but by piled-up sand.

The mountain of Torgat in Norway is pierced from top to bottom by a huge gap. Here is the story of its origins: a Jutul or giant fell in love with a maiden, but she, skilled in magic, rejected his love and even changed his love letters into stone. The exasperated giant drew his bow in revenge, and his mighty arrow flew through the air and passed through the mountain, leaving the gap that can be seen to this day. The arrow did not quite reach its target but fell at the feet of the maiden on the island of Lekoë, where it still remains in the shape of a huge, tall rock. By means of spells the giant and the maiden turned each other to stone, so they stand facing each other until Judgement Bay. Even nowadays no Norwegian sailor passes by without taking off his cap to salute the maiden of Lekoë.

One day when St. Olaf was sailing close by the high hills on the coast of Horns Herred, a giantess who lived there cried: "St. Olaf with the red beard, you are passing too close to the walls of my cellar." St. Olaf flew into a rage and instead of steering his ship between the cliffs, he turned the ship's head to the hills and replied: "Listen, you with the distaff and the spindle, you shall remain where you are and be turned to stone." Hardly had he finshed speaking when the giantess was changed into a rock. This can still be seen on the eastern cliff, and it does indeed have something like a distaff and a spindle.

On Cap Fréhel in Northern Brittany there some large rocks known as *Les Pierres dérublées* (Fallen Stones). Long ago there was a house on that spot. Its inhabitants incurred the anger of some local fairies, who in revenge tumbled these rocks down onto the house on the wedding-day of the family's eldest son.

When the cliffs have a distinct coloring such as red, popular imagination sees the cause as the fabulous work of heroes, monsters or gigantic ships. The sailors of North Frisia tell that one day the great ship Mannigfual entered the Straits of Dover. Because of the narrowness of the strait it was impossible to pass between Dover and Calais, so the captain had the good idea of smearing the port side with soap. Thanks to this Mannigfual passed through without any damage and entered the North Sea. Ever since those days the cliffs of Dover are as white as soap because of the great ship and the lather it left in passing. According to Danish folklore the Cliff King walks along the cliffs of Moen, Stevn and Rügen. He drives a strange chariot drawn by four black horses, galloping from cliff to cliff across the sea, which is whipped up by his progress. There is also the story of a cliff giant who twice saved the country from its enemies by changing all the stones on the shore into mounted warriors.

When Hawaii is threatened by disaster, doleful cries can be heard near a certain rock. This bears the name Kavere-Hea in memory of an innocent woman who was thrown over the cliffs by her husband and fell to her death on that very rock. While falling she protested her innocence and forgave her murderer. Since then several Hawaians have reported seeing her shade flitting over the waves or hearing plaintive cries.

The cliffs of Cornwall, particularly where shipwreck has taken place, provide the setting for ghosts. A fisherman or pilot who as out walking one night along the sands of Porth Towan heard a voice from the sea cry, "The hour has come, but not the man". This was repeated three times, then a dark figure resembling a man rushed along the cliff and fell into the sea. This story is told in various forms all along the Cornish coast.

From time immemorial popular imagination has peopled caves along the coast with spirits and divinities. In the *Odyssey* Ulysses and his companions draw their ship up on the beach and leave it in a vast cave which nymphs use for their songs and dances.

On the Island of St. Vincent the Caribbeans say that a dreaded siren lived in a cave hollowed out in the rocks of the southern shore.

In Cornwall a cleft in the rocks near Portreath known as Ralph's Cupboard was the home of the giant Wrath who watched for ships being driven onto his part of the coast, strode out into the sea to tie them to his belt and devoured the fishermen in them.

In Scandinavia the giants also lived in caves. Near the Queen's Seat on the cliffs of Moen there is a cavern high above the high water mark which used to be the home of the Giant of Uppsala. One day a brave man decided to go and see the giant in his cave. He climbed down a rope to the cave and was never seen again. One of the caves in this cliff was the home of Jon Opsal himself, the other served as the stable for his horse.

At Ploubazlanec in Northern Brittany they say that in the last century the fishermen of Loguivy were terrified of the sea-witches who used to live in a cave called Toul ar Groac'h, a short distance away across from the little port. When they returned at night, rather than pass this haunted spot, they used to turn their boats over on the beach and sleep underneath them. But it seems that the sea-witches had no power over women, for when these walked ahead of their menfolk, the latter were not afraid and followed them past the witches' caves.

A cave on the island of Croagez near Port-Blanc in Brittany was once inhabited by a sea-fairy (Groac'h Vor). A woman passing the spot one night saw a light shining in the hollow of the rocks. She went into the cave and saw an old woman spinning. The old woman, a fairy in disguise, gave her a distaff, saying that if she spoke to no-one of her discovery she would be given great riches. When she returned home she was curious to try out the distaff and began to spin. For month after month the distaff spun fine thread which she sold at a good price, while her stock of wool remained undiminished. She would doubt-less have made her fortune if her tongue had not led her astray, but one day one of her neighbors asked why she had such an abundance of fine thread and she told her visit to the fairy. From that very moment the distaff lost its magic powers, and the money that she had amassed disappeared as well.

The theme of a magic gift which disappears when it is spoken of is very common in the legends of Upper Brittany.

In his *History of the Goths* Olaüs Magnus writes that along the coast of the North Sea there are measureless caverns from which come fearsome, unearthly howls made by sea-monsters hideous to describe.

In Wide Bay can be seen the mouth of the little river Burnett. The local colored people say that in the deep cave nearby lives a dreadful being which would seize them if they passed by. Not far away there is a lagoon which local people refuse to go near because of superstitious dread.

Capes, straits, bays and natural harbors

Many capes have names derived from their shapes. They are often called "heads", and Valmont-Bomare even quotes the latter as a synonym. In countries where Celtic languages are or were spoken, there are a number of capes whose names begin with the prefix *pen* (head) such as Penmar'h in Finistère, Penhap, Pen-Boc'h in Morbihan, Pen-Bwch in Wales, Penclos in Anglesey, Pentire in Cornwall.

The term *nez* (nose) is even more widespread. On the coast of the Pas-de-Calais there are Cornez, Gris-nez and Blanc-nez; the latter having its counterpart in Scotland: White-Ness. In Normandy Nez de Carteret, and Nez de Jobourg also denote capes, as does Gros-Nez in Jersey. In his *History of the Normans* Depping is of the opinion that these place-names come from the word *noesse*, a Scandinavian term for cape. Hence the chieftains who had settled on them called themselves *Noesse-Kongar*, or Kings of the Capes. In England and Scotland the suffix *-ness* is used for many headlands such as Holderness, Oxfordness, Dungeness, Whiteness. This image comes so easily to the mind of English mariners that they give the name *Sweet-nose* to Cape Svioeloe Nose (Holy Cape) in the White Sea.

In Brittany the names of certain headlands have the prefix *Fri* or *Fré*, meaning "nose": Fréhel, Frinandour. Several capes also bear the name *le Grouin*. According to Bruce, a headland in the Red Sea which is thought to ressemble a nose was called by the Arabs *Ras-el-Anf*, or Cape of the Nose. In Japan there are two rocks, one of which projects out over the sea. One is called The Man's Nose *(Me Oga Fana)*. The other nose-shaped rock bears the name of *Soto Fana*.

Sayings about headlands often contain the idea of danger:

He who lives on a headland needs to be a good swimmer (Arab).

Doubler le cap or *doubler la pointe* (French) means literally "rounding the cape" but implies overcoming a difficulty.

In French slang *doubler un cap* means to make a detour to avoid someone to whom one owes money.

In ports of call where sailors go ashore to sample the local amusements, they call the quarter which houses the taverns, bars and brothels "Cape Horn".

In the South of Africa in the dry season of the year a mass of white cloud hangs over Table Mountain and Devil's Peak. It is thought to cause the terrible South-East winds which blow off the Cape of Good Hope. When sailors see these clouds they say, "The table is laid" or "The table cloth is on". Le Vaillant says that the local inhabitants have a saying, "We shall have wind, Table Mountain is wearing its wig."

Like cliffs, capes sometimes owe their origins to gods or heroes. In the *Lusiad* Adamastor is changed by the anger of the gods into a headland, a metamorphosis perhaps not entirely invented by Camoens. In Canto V we find the words: "From my dry flesh and my bones turned to rocks the inflexible gods made the headland which juts into the vast sea, and to increase my sufferings and insult my grief the moist girdle of Thetis oppresses me every day".

Headlands inspired a religious devotion which showed itself in the building of temples, the making of offerings and in prayers. When writing of the tomb of Themistocles, Plutarch says: "Set in an open place, your tomb is saluted by mariners entering or leaving the harbor." In classical times certain capes were greatly feared. One such was Cape Malè: an ancient proverb said: "When you round Cape Malè, forget the name of your fatherland." In the icy northern seas there are many "svatöi nos" or holy capes. Sailors round them with great anxiety, wondering whether they may not be seized by wind or current or lose their way in fog on the other side of the point.

Amongst the headlands most feared by mariners is the Bec du Raz in Finistère. Its sinister reputation can be judged from the large number of local sayings.

When certain winds are blowing, the sailors of St. Malo say: "In this weather, even God could not round the Bec du Raz".

"Nobody passes round Raz without misfortune or terror".

"If you round the Bec du Raz, if you don't die you will tremble with fear".

"He who does not steer a good course round Raz will surely perish".

Sailors say the following prayer when passing the cape:

"O God, protect me rounding the Bec du Raz,

For my ship is small and your sea is vast".

It was also the custom to say one's prayers when passing to the north of Ushant. No Breton sailor ever rounded St. Nicolas' point without singing the hymn *Ave Maris Stella* and calling on St. Nicolas to protect him from the dangerous currents.

In past centuries, when ships passed safely round certain headlands, prayers of thanksgiving were said for safe deliverance. When the Manilla Galleon sighted Cape Espiritu Santo on the coast of California the *Te Deum* was sung.

Dangerous straits are sometimes given vivid names. One near Ushant is called *Le Fromveur* (Great Fear). Because of its treacherous currents le Helder is also called *Porte d'Enfer* (Gate of Hell). *Bab-el-Mandeb* means Gate of Affliction.

The mountains of Calpe and Abile were once joined, but Hercules separated them and opened up the strait which gives access to the Atlantic. The demigod Rupe separated North Island from South Island, New Zealand, directing the sea through Cook Strait and cutting New Zealand in two.

St. Olaf, finding the sea route he normally used on his visits too long, steered a straight course. The land opened up before him, forming a strait still known as Cross Strait.

Norwegian folklore gives St. Olaf as the origin of various straits. According to one Norwegian legend the mountains of Hornelen were once joined to Moroë. St. Olaf headed for them and ordered them to separate to let him pass, thus creating the strait which divides them to this day.

The current called *Mosko Strom* or Maelstrom was believed by mariners to be the dwelling-place of an octopus with tentacles hundred of yards long whipping up the waters into an immense whirlpool which sucked in and ungulfed ships. This ancient legend is the source of the idea that the Maelstrom is a sort of funnel-shaped abyss which ships approach in ever-narrowing circles until finally they plunge into its whirling depths.

In classical times people thought that the depths of the Straits of Messina were the "navel of the sea". They also believed that the sides of these straits came together to intercept, smash and engulf ships, then separated again—a fiction which is probably the result of the ancient travellers' astonishment and fear rather than a mere embellishment for a tale.

Bays have a variety of shapes, some form almost a semi-circle, others make a deep, strangely-curved indentation in the shore line.

Like many estuaries and rivers, bays used to demand an annual victim: every year the bay of Kiel required a human sacrifice. Evil spirits had their hiding-places there, and they demanded a human life as the price for allowing a ship a safe passage. Once the Isse Fjord was inhabited by a Troll. It was his custom to stop every ship entering the fjord and demand a man. Seafarers put up with this calamity until news came that the Troll would lose his power when shown the head of Pope Lucius, who had lived in Rome several centuries before. Monks were sent to fetch it, and when their ship returned the Troll appeared as usual. But when the monks the monks held up the head of the pope, he let out a horrible cry and was turned to stone.

In the bay of Ambon a huge fish lives near the mole and every year carries off one victim.

Snakes which coil up on heaps of gold to hatch out their young are said to live on the beds of Iceland's deepest lakes, fjords and bays. They have been seen spewing up their venom onto the shore.

It is believed that in the Baie des Trépassés at the extreme tip of Brittany on All Souls' Day one can hear the groans of shipwrecked sailors from each wave. The souls of the local fishermen lost at sea gather in this spot.

We associate harbors with security and calm. In France they say of a good man who has died and gone to Heaven: "il est arrivé au port" ("he has reached harbor"). Philosophers of long ago used to speak of death as a destination to be reached at the end of a long journey and compared life to a voyage over a sea full of dangerous reefs.

In one of Sir Water Scott's stories sailors drink to a dead shipmate, wishing him a good voyage and a safe arrival in port.

In Italy *porto termine* is a synonym for death. *Essere in porto* means to have reached the end. In French slang *le havre* (literally "the great harbor") means "God".

Et miserarium portus est patientia (Patience is the port of misery).

Portus optimus poenitenti mutatio consilii (Cicero: The best port for a penitent is to change his way of life).

In French *arriver à bon port, s'assurer un port, attraper un port*, all imply reaching safety after facing many dangers.

In one of Alexandre Dumas' books there is the following passage: "He would have liked to set a course, with the wind behind him, for the safe anchorage of matrimony. Henoque had given me his Bible oath that he would find a good mooring in his native village and would pay out a hundred fathoms of cable rather than drag his anchor in the storms and tide-races of civilian life".

The French idiom *se mettre à quai*, like its English equivalent "being on the beach" is the mariner's term for retirement from the sea.

Harbors have sometimes been likened to a stable, an image based on a comparison between ships and horses: "Just as a horse returning from the open fields enters his stable, so does a ship returning from the sea enter its harbor as a place of safety."

Dreams about a seaport mean profit, good news, happiness.

In Rome the goddess Mater Matuta presided over harbors, like the Greek Leucothoë, with whom she was later identified.

Legends generally ascribe to harbors the same origins as bays. Here is one which explains the name given to a little fishing port called Spern-en-Trelevern to the west of Port-Blanc: one day the fishermen of this and neighboring ports were surprised by the English. They hastily weighed anchor and sailed back to the little cove which is nowadays Porz-spern. The English pursued them but soon found themselves in the middle of a thorn thicket from which they could not escape and perished to a man. This is what gave the place its name—Porz-Spern (Port of Thorns).

Greenland folklore tells that the port of Godhav'n is the notch to which was tied the strap used by a magician to move the island of Disco to its present position.

Sands and the beaches

In places where there are no cliffs to form the shoreline, rolling sand-dunes extend back into the interior, often for miles.

Some of these sandbanks move a considerable distance each year, especially where no conifers have been planted to hold them fast. This is the meaning of an ancient saying about sand-dunes of the Charente coast quoted by Reclus: "In Arvert the mountains walk."

In Nordstrand there lived a mermaid who pastured her cattle on the shore. This displeased the peasants of the neighborhood, who captured her and her cattle and told her that they would not let her go until she had paid for the use of the pastures. As she replied that she had no money, they demanded the belt she was wearing, a fine thing set with precious stones. She gave it to them as a ransom for her cattle. But while leading her cattle back she called to her bull, which began to dig its horns into the ground and throw sand into the air. As the wind was from the north-west, the sand was blown towards the village of Tibirke, whose church was almost buried beneath it. As for the beautiful belt, when its new owners got it home they found it was made of old rushes.

According to a folktale from Holstein (Grimm, *Deutsche Märchen*) a holy woman was once walking along the shore, looking up into the heavens and praying. The people of the village, out and about that Sunday afternoon dressed in their best clothes, met her and made fun of her piety. She paid no attention to them and prayed to God asking him not to hold this sin against them. But the next morning two bulls came and spent the whole day churning up with their horns a large sandhill which lay nearby. When night fell a high wind blew the sand from the sandhill onto the village and buried it completely. Every living thing died. When the people of neighboring villages arrived and tried to dig out the buried village, all their work was filled in during the night. So the village remains buried to this day.

In Upper Brittany certain sandbanks are said to be the haunts of fairies who dislike being disturbed.

In Cornwall sailors tell of having seen on the beach at night men who do not reply when spoken to. They have wrinkled hands like those of women who have been doing their washing, and the water squelches in their boots when they walk. They follow the sailors without answering a word.

It is said that skeletons swathed in white roam at night over lonely beaches. These are the souls of shipwrecked sailors seeking their parents.

The inhabitants of the island of Arz say that they have sometimes seen the white shapes of women coming from neighboring islands or from the mainland. They walk over the sea and huddle sad-faced on the shore, where they dig out the sand with their bare feet and pluck the leaves off the sprigs of rosemary they have picked on the beach. They are the daughters of the island who have rashly married strangers, died in sin far from their native soil and then returned to beg friends and relatives to pray for their souls.

An English legend versified by Charles Kingsley in *The Sands of Dee*, tells of a girl lost in the fog, surprised by the tide and drowned in the rising waters. Ever since

"The boatmen hear her call the cattle home
Across the sands of Dee".

In Tahiti all the beaches planted with casuarinas, gloomy trees which talk at night, are said to be haunted by the souls of drowned men who come to weep there.

On the coast near Yport in Normandy sea-horses and sea-sheep often appear on the beaches, their eyes having such hypnotic influence that careless people who meet their glance are drawn irresistibly towards the sea, in which they disappear for ever.

People speak of sand to convey the idea of huge, immeasurable quantity:

The Bretons talk of someone "telling as many lies as there are grains of sand.¨

¨If my troubles and grief were weighed on scales they would weigh more than the sands of the sea¨ (Job).

¨My sufferings are as innumerable as the sands of the sea¨ (Aristophanes, *The Acharnians*).

¨It would be as difficult to count the labors of Hercules as to number the sands of the sea¨ (Pindar).

The Latins borrowed from the Greeks the proverb *Arenam metiris*—¨to measure the sands¨—meaning an impossible task (Erasmus).

Mere end Stierner paa Himelen, Sand i Havet (More than the stars in the sky and the grains of sand in the sea—Danish).

¨Favors are granted in vain to those who are unworthy, it is like writing on the sands of the sea¨ (Tamil).

Ex arena funiculum nectis (Erasmus). ¨He is making ropes of sand¨ (English)—these imply doing useless work.

A legend reported in the *Revue britannique* is relevant to this proverbial saying. It tells of one Michael Scott, whose invisible spirit-helpers demanded ever more work to do. He ordered them to make ropes of sand. When they asked to be allowed to add a little straw, he refused and the spirits are laboring at their task to this day.

Arare litus (To plough the shore—Erasmus).

Arenae mandas semina (to sow the sands with seed—Erasmus).

He is sowing on the sand (Boun).

In arena aedificas (to build on sand—Erasmus).

Since classical times sand from the sea-shore has been thought to have curative powers Pliny says that when it is fine-grained and warmed by the sun it is excellent for drying out the bodies of patients suffering from dropsy and rheumatism.

This method is also used in the Pacific. The inhabitants of the Marquesas consider sandbaths an excellent way of developing children's muscles. About three o'clock in the afternoon, when the beach has been well warmed by the sun, a hole is dug in the sand and the child is buried in it up to his armpits.

In the Tréguier region, when children suffer from colic, sand is heated up, put in little bags and placed on their stomachs.

In Algeria sea-sand was also used, not as a medicine but as a kind of ordeal. Often devoted mothers used to bury their children up to their necks in sea-sand for several hours. They believed that those who survived this ordeal would have a long and happy life.

In his *Bride of Lammermoor* Sir Walter Scott writes of quicksands known as "the Kilpie's Flow". These are uncovered by the tide and trap people, who disappear for ever when the tide comes in. The last of the Ravenswoods died there, fulfilling a prophesy made by Thomas the Rhymer.

Near the Mont Saint-Michel in Normandy people tell the story of a family returning from a pilgrimage there who were sucked in by quicksands. The husband held up his wife with one hand and his son with the other to keep them from going under. Just when they were about to be sucked down an angel appeared, took the boy's hand and pulled all three to safety.

Reefs

Simple, unsophisticated people often invent supernatural causes for things which amaze or frightens them. Many rocks, because of their strange shape, enormous size and the dangers they present to seafaress, do not look as if they had been created naturally by the action of the waves, movements of the earth and other physical causes. Popular imagination has invented gods and spirits to place them in position, and legends tell how it happened.

In Finnish folklore Luonnotar, mother of the waves, passes over the sea and spawns reefs to cause the death of sailors. On the coast of Yorkshire the devil built the Bridge of Filey to wreck ships.

Neptune scattered reefs all over the Aegean when he hurled them in his battle against the giants. The Hawains still point out the rocks hurled by Pele, goddess of volcanoes, at Chief Kahavari's canoe when he fled from her anger.

In Brittany there are many rocks which are said to have been shaken out of a giant's shoe. Others are the giant's dung. Others were said to be the missiles he hurled at enemies or birds.

According to a Baltic tradition the rock known as *Moensknit* (Maiden's Rock) is a beautiful young fairy who rules over the island and waters round it. The white parts are her robes falling in folds down to the level of the sea. She protects seafarers, especially fishermen. At night melodious voices are heard from the waves around the rock. These are the voices of other fairies paying homage to their queen.

In Tahiti a rock, called the Accursed Rock, overhangs a road. Once it was condemned by Taroa, the creator of the world, to move for ever at the mercy of the waves and never to find a nesting-place on earth. After centuries of ceaseless movement it caught sight of Tahiti. Tü, Goddess of the Night, seeing that it wished to rest there, told it that Taroa could not see what happened at night and advised it to stop there and roll itself in mud so that Taroa would not recognise it. One morning it was surprised by the dawn, and Taroa hurled a bolt of lightning at it. It remained under a curse, and those who fall asleep in its shade never wake up again.

At times rocks rise up from the sea-bed to come to the aid of heroes in danger. A fairy who was crossing from Jersey to Val André grew tired and needed a rest. In her shoe was a pebble which was troubling her, so she took her shoe off and shook it. The pebble fell into the sea and grew so much in size that the fairy was able to sit down on it and take a rest. This is now the Verdelet rock near Pleneuf (Côtes-du-Nord). In an Irish legend a hero went out on to a rock in the sea to do penance. The rock swelled in size and soon formed an island. Danish folklore tells of a rock which rose up to aid a heroine fleeing from danger. Helen, Princess of Scania, was pursued by a king who hated her and fled for her life. Just as the king was about to catch her she came to the shore. She threw herself into the sea, but was not drowned, as a large rock rose up from the bottom of the sea to save her. In another version of the story the princess was thrown into the sea, but was rescued by the rock and brought to Seeland.

In the *Odyssey* Neptune flew into a rage at the ship which brought Ulysses back to Ithaca and turned it into a rock.

It was once believed that St. Maclou lived on the great rock known as Ortach, which stands in the sea between Aurigny and the Casquets. Many old sailors said they had seen him from a distance sitting and reading a book. Passing sailors used to make a genuflection before this rock until in modern times it was discovered that the rock's inhabitant was a devil named Jochmus, who had been passing himself off as St. Maclou for centuries (Victor Hugo, *Les Travailleurs de la mer*). Coast-dwellers believe that the seagulls which fly around reefs are men who have died in shipwreck there and whose corpses rest in the depths of the ocean.

In the Pacific two gods who were very strict about being shown a proper

respect lived in palace on some rocks. At the mouth of the Gambia River in Africa there are two sacred rocks inhabited by the god of the sea and the waves. The sailors of the *Cossack*, showing little respect for the rocks, struck them with hammers. The local natives warned them that they would anger the god, but they paid no attention. When the *Cossack* was passing the bar the god slipped underneath the ship. Dancing with rage, he made the ship bob about like a cork. The captain let down his anchors, but the enraged god cut the anchor-cables and shook the vessel until it broke up. When Marsden visited the Gambia River the natives begged him not to risk death by touching the rocks.

At the beginning of the 16th century Baron von Herbestein was travelling in the Baltic. When trying to sail round a rocky mountain his ship was held up by contrary winds. A mariner told the captain: "The rock you see is called Semes, and if you not appease it by an offering, we shall not be able to sail beyond it." The captain rebuked him for his vain superstition, and after they had been held up for three or four days, the wind suddenly dropped, and they weighed anchor. When a fair wind sprang up to carry them further on their voyage, the sailor said: "You laughed at me when I spoke of appeasing the rock of Semes, and treated the idea as vain superstition. But if I had not secretly prayed to the rock during the night and gained its favor you would not have got very far". When asked what offering he had made, he said that he had spread flour mixed with butter on the rock.

Similar practices are found amongst primitive tribes, especially in America and Africa. Here are two examples chosen from many: on the Huron trail near Quebec there are rocks which are especially venerated. The Hurons never fail to make offerings when they pass along the trail to trade their goods. They believe that a demon dwells in the hollow of the rocks who can make their journey successful. That is why they stop and make offerings, which they simply place in one of the crevices in the rock, addressing the following prayer to it: "Spirit who dwells in this spot, here are my offerings which I give you. Help us, guard us from shipwreck and grant that, having made good trade, we shall return safe and sound to our village" (*Rélations des Juésuites*, 1636).

In the Mafa River in West Africa there is a dangerous rock near which all passers-by leave an offering for the spirit of the waters. This offering consists of a handful of rice or a glass of rum.

Sandbanks and islands

Sandbanks can lie at various depths, but most of them are just below the surface and thus are as much feared by sailors as reefs.

English and American mariners have a name for those sandbanks which lie in very shallow water and make the waves break over them: they call them "frying pans". Of all the sandbanks they are the most dangerous.

The sandbanks off the coast of Belgium and Holland were dreaded by Spanish sailors. The dangers they represented and the skill needed to survive them gave rise to the proverbial expression used in *Don Quixote:* "capable of passing through the Flemish sandbanks", a term of high praise meaning clever and skilled.

Legends about sandbanks are rather like those about rocks. In a Dutch folktale a lady of Stavoren asked one of her sea-captains to bring back whatever he thought most valuable. He returned with a cargo of wheat, but the lady had it thrown into the harbor. Where it sank a large sandbank formed, which was known as the *Frauensand* (Lady's Sands). The sandbank grew till it blocked the harbor and made it unusable (Grimm, *Deutsche Märchen*).

The sea, in isolating islands from the mainland and surrounding them by waves, invests them with a kind of mystery. They are the subject of countless legends which tell of their supernatural origins. Hawaians tell of earliest times when the ocean covered the world. A huge bird laid an egg which, doubtless fertilised by the sun, formed the island of Hawaii. This egg legend is common to many parts of the world.

Elsewhere folklore tells of islands deriving directly from gods. A Japanese folk-tale tells how many islands were born of the union of Isanaghi and Isanami. Tahitian mythology relates that the god Etua-Rahaï threw his wife O-Te-Tapad into the sea. She (who is fact the primordial rock) broke into pieces and formed the reefs and islands scattered over the ocean.

According to traditions common to the classical times and countries whose existence the Greeks and Romans never dreamed of, the gods sometimes raised up islands to come to the aid of persecuted divinities or heroes in peril.

There is legend that the island of Delos emerged from the waters to give refuge to Latona. The island floated at first, but was later supported by four columns which had risen from the sea-bed to anchor it in place.

Malayan folklore tells that in the beginning there was only sky and water and a kite flying between them. Then the sky cast an island into the sea to make a resting place for the bird.

A certain author writes that Maui went out fishing with his brothers, who let down their nets and brought up a good catch of fish. When Maui wanted to start fishing he asked them for bait. They refused to give him any, so he baited his hook with his own blood and threw it into the sea. The hook sank down to the bottom and caught onto the house of old Tonganui. Maui pulled on his line, the sea boiled all around the boat, and Maui's brothers grumbled, while he himself sang a magic song to bring the fish up easily from the sea. At the end of his song he saw his fish floating on the surface—part of the land of Papa-tu-a-Nuku.

The Maoris tell another legend. One day old Morm was fishing from a rock and felt something immovable at the end of his line. This was surprising, for usually he had no difficulty in catching even whales. As he could not get the end of his line out of the water, he tied it to a pigeon's feet. Breathing his spirit into the bird, he told it to fly into the air. When it did, New Zealand rose above the waters.

A folk-tale which is found in Greece, Scandinavia and the Pacific tells how islands were created from clods of earth thrown into the sea by heroes or demigods. Jason ordered Euphymus to throw the Libyan land given him by Triton in the sea. There it formed the island of Calliste.

Snorri's Edda relates that Gylfe, king of Sweden, granted a young lady as much land as four oxen could plow in a day. She yoked oxen of gigantic size to the plough, but the plowshare bit so deeply into the land that it broke away a part, which fell into the sea and became the island of Seeland.

Nordic sailors have a number a semi-humorous stories about the origins of various islands, telling how they were caused by the passing of a huge ship. According to the Frisian legend an enormous vessel had entered the Baltic, but the crew immediately saw that the water was too shallow. To get more water under her keel they threw ballast, ashes and garbage overboard. The island of Bornholm was formed from the ballast and the little island of Christiansö from the rest. Other islands, were formed when one day the cook the legendary ship Refanu was making lentil soup and threw the lentil pods overboard. Twice Refanu was forced to jettison ballast, which made the islands of Euland and Gotland.

According to other folk-tales, certain islands left their original positions and moved to new ones often far away.

In ancient times the island of Disco lay well to the South, close up against the coast of Greenland. Its position blocked the Greenlanders' access to the open sea, much to their disgust. Two great magicians got together to tow the hated island away, but a third opposed their plan. The two magicians launched their kayaks in the sea, tied the island to them with a fine hair from the head of a child and would have moved the island away without any trouble if the other magician had not held it back with a sealskin thong. The struggle was a long one. Bent over their paddles the magicians churned furiously, chanting spells and pulling on the hair. But their lone opponent held on grimly to his thong, straining every muscle against them. Suddenly to his amazement, the thong parted and the island floated to the north, where the two magicians ordered it to stop. The second folk-tale tells that Disco once lay opposite the Baal River and that a magician managed to move it to its present position by using a magic strap.

The Kurile people, tell the following tale about an uninhabited island near their shore. It used to be in the middle of Lake Kurile on the point of Kamchatka, but as it shaded nearby mountains these made war on it and forced it to move elsewhere. It was sick at heart at having to leave its beloved lake and as a mark of its affection left behind its heart. To this day there is a rock in the lake known as the Heart Rock. To repay its affection the lake followed it,

scooping out a path to the sea which nowadays the bed of the River Ozern-aia.

According to the legend Ireland floated on the waters during the Deluge.

In the Middle Ages people believed that St. Brendan's Isle used to hide itself slyly from eyes of seafarers, allowing itself to be glimpsed from time to time.

A tradition common along the North Sea coast told of floating islands which used to emerge from the waves. They had full-grown trees with branches covered in sea-shells instead of leaves. After a few hours they would submerge again.

Ordinary people and sailors thought these were the under-sea dwellings of evil spirits who brought them to the surface to make fun of seafarers, confuse their navigation and increase the difficulties of their voyages. The geographer Ruraeus marked one of these, Gummer's Ore, on his map. It used to appear amongst the reefs off Stockholm. Baron Grippenheim tells that he looked for the island in vain until one day he happened to turn his head and saw what looked like three dots suddenly rising out of the sea. "That's Gummer's Ore, isn't it?" he asked the helmsman of his boat. "I don't know, but you can be sure that what we see foretells a storm or a good catch of fish," the other replied. Gummer's Ore is no more than a tangle of reefs just below the surface of the sea.

Other Norwegian folk-tales tell of enchanted floating islands. Far out to sea opposite Troenon in the Heligoland, Strait there is a sandbank known as Sandfloesen. It is an excellent place for fishing but is difficult to find, because it moves from one place to another.

This sandbank has not always been at the bottom of the sea. In ancient times it was an island owned by a rich Heligoland farmer. He had put up a hut to live in in the summertime. Some say that this sandbank sometimes comes to the surface looking like a lovely island. But passing sailors and fishermen used to tell of hearing shouts of laughter, music, dancing and all kinds of hullabaloo coming from it, as if a ship's crew were making merry on the island. Sailors lost no time in getting as far away as possible. Nobody ever saw a living soul on Sandfloesen.

Once every few years early Bostonians used to be treated to an unusual sight. On a clear calm day in the Fall an island covered in greenery used to surface to the East. The island was so distinct in its shape and colors that nobody could doubt its existence. Its story goes back to the days when the early settlers first caugh sight of it. They launched their boats to investigate, but a storm blew up and wrecked them just whem they were hoisting sail to reach the island, which seemed to recede before them. Since then no white man ever succeeded in reaching it. Sometimes it seemed to recede as fast as people approached. At other times it stayed quite still until the boats nearly touched it, but then the sun would suddenly be obscured, plunging them in darkness. An Indian, the last of his tribe, sighted it just before his death, and he launched his canoe "to go to the Island of the Happy Spirits", as he put it. He disappeared a terrible storm, and since then the island has never been seen again.

Many years ago the name *Butter Island* was given to an island which was said to appear in the Atlantic. It was sighted from time to time, but it always disappeared again very quickly. It was said to melt away like a lump of butter.

A Tahitian told Captain Cook about an island inhabited by huge giants as tall as a mainmast and as thick as a capstan-head. They are usually mild-tempered, but when they are angry with someone they pick him up and throw him out to sea like a pebble. They are so big that they could carry Cook's ship on their backs.

From classical times onwards poets, perhaps inspired by seafarers' tales, mention islands inhabited only by women. They welcome sailors and entertain them to thoroughly with sensual delights that they forget all about the perils of the sea and the port they are bound for.

When one reads of the early voyages made by Europeans to the Pacific, one realises how much these sailors were delighted by the liberal and uninhibited amorousness of the women of the South Seas and the permissiveness of their menfolk. From there it was but a short step to omit all mention of the harmless males and idealise the hospitale womenfolk, as is so often done in the enthusiastic 19th century descriptions of Tahiti and other amoral islands.

According to Apollonius, Jason's Argonauts were detained for several days on Lemnos, where the women had got rid of their husbands by murdering them. The Danish hero Olger Danske was held captive by a fairy on an enchanted island, as Ulysses was by Calypso and as happened to many other heroes. Arab geographers called certain islands the "Isles of the Immortal Maidens", which implies a legend like that of the Argonauts. One island, Geziret el Nessa, is inhabited only by women. Not only are there no men, there are no male animals of any kind. On one of these islands the women and animals are fertilised by a wind which blows on a certain day once a year. On the other fertilisation results from eating the fruit of certain trees.

The Fijians used to tell of a neighboring island where only women were to be found. They had the gift of immortality but also all the passions of ordinary women.

Arab folklore mentions islands with individual peculiarities. The forests which cover the island of Wak are made up of strange trees whose branches and foliage enclose the armless and legless torsos of women hanging by their hair.

In his *De Bello Gothico* Procopius relates that the souls of the dead were taken by boat to the island of Britia. This tradition is still found in Brittany. Around Tréguier people believe that boats carry the souls of the dead, and especially those drowned at sea, to unknown islands which human eyes have never seen. They exist nevertheless and will appear when the world comes to an end. On summer evenings when the wind drops and the sea is calm, one can see white shapes hovering around these black boats and hear the creaking of their oars. If anyone tries to follow them out to sea, he has to follow them for ever.

Of Newfoundland there is an Island called Deadman Islet, said to be a place of refuge for the souls of those lost at sea. Nobody dares approach it for fear of falling under their spell.

Other peoples locate their Elysian Fields on various islands: in this respect ancient European and Indian traditions agree with those of mediaeval Celts and present-day Polynesians. Hesiod writes that after the death of heroes at the siege of Troy "the mighty son of Saturn, giving them nourishment and a dwelling-place different from those of other men, placed them on the fringes of the world. These happy heroes inhabit the Fortunate Islands on the other side of the ocean's vasty deeps, and three times a year the fertile soil yields them glossy fruit as sweet as honey." This tradition is singularly like one reported by Macpherson and quoted by Tylor which says that after they die, heroes go to Flatt-Innis, the home of the dead, perpetually green and lush, calm and serene even when the Atlantic is stormy.

Pindar has this to say of the island of the dead: "Those whose souls have lived thrice on earth and thrice in the underworld and are innocent of all wrongdoings, are taken to the city of Saturn by the route traced by Jupiter. This city lies in the middle of the ocean, on an island refreshed by the sweet breath of the zephyrs and adorned with a thousand golden flowers". This was the source from which Plato derived his allegory of Atlantis.

Not all magic islands were the dwelling-places of the dead or gods. Some had magic fountains whose water conferred immortality on those lucky enough to make their way there despite all obstacles.

Diodorus Siculus describes a large island in the middle of the sea which enjoys perpetual spring and is the home of gods rather than mortals.

Gaelic folklore speaks of wonderful, far-off countries called in pagan days *Traig* (Great Shore), *Tir nam-Beo* (Land of the Living), *Mag Mell* (Plain of Delights), *Flaith Innis* (Island of Heroes). In the Christian epoch they were called *Taingire* (St. Brendan's Promised Land). Then in Ossianic poetry they became *Tir-nan-Og* or *Tir ha hoge* (Lands of Days, or Land of Youth).

Sea-shells,
pebbles, seaweed

In Algeria sea-shells are considered one of the most powerful amulets. Lapplanders still throw sea-shells known as *dogs' souls* into the graves of their dogs.

Strabo writes that the women of the Troglodytes who lived in the coast of Africa wore sea-shells around their necks to guard against evil spells.

In Calabria sea-shells are used against the Evil Eye. In Asturias nursing mothers used to wear a certain type of sea-shell *(cuenta de la leche)* round their necks to make their milk more plentiful. When they wanted the flow of milk to cease they had only to throw the sea-shells over their shoulders. This kind of amulet needs to be gathered from the sea if it is to be effective.

In Dacca there is an entire industry devoted to the making of bracelets, pendants and amulets of all kinds from the shells of *Turbinella pyrum* and *Turbinella rapa*. Occasionally one comes across a sinistral shell, a sacred object which is considered to bring luck to its owner. One of these fetched the equivalent of four thousand dollars in Calcutta in 1882. This idea of a sacred, luck-bringing shell is not peculiar to Hindus. It was even more popular in classical times. Aelianus writes that whirlwinds have a king whose every command they obey. The fishermen lucky enough to capture this king will succeed in everything he undertakes, and even those present when the king is found are sure of good fortune. In Byzantium the man who made such a catch was rewarded—all the other fishermen gave him a drachma. It is certainly strange to find this same legend of the finding of a sacred luck-bringing shell amongst two peoples so different from each other.

The sacred sinistral shell does not exist only in the imagination of ancient authors of Hindu religious works. Though rare, they are sometimes found in the sea. They have always been diligently sought by fishermen. A Brahminic legend tells that one of the companions who went with Rana on his journey to Ceylon was forced to take refuge from a demon by entering a Xanxus shell whose whorl turned from left to right. On the anniversary of that event devout Brahmins come to Tuticorin to try and catch this very Xanxus.

Pebbles found on the beach figure in folk-belief and superstitions. In the New Hebrides natives venerate certain pebbles washed by the sea. In the Bay of Johore blue and white pebbles are believed to be sacred: to take them away is an unforgivable sacrilege, punished by immediate shipwreck. These phenomena are linked with the worship of stones which is so widespread in all parts of the world. In India one finds similar beliefs relating to gods using pebbles as dwelling-places.

During storms the pebbles of the shingle which lies thick round the shores of Sept-Iles (North Brittany) rub together, making a noise which can be heard for miles. It is quite distinct from the sound of the sea breaking on the rocks. The islanders and people of the coast have a saying which reflects the terror inspired by this sound: "At night on Sept-Iles, when the weather is rough, you can hear the stones talk."

At Plouezec near Paimpol many years ago the parish priest used to bless white pebbles from one of the local beaches. Sailors used to put them in little canvas bags and wear them on their chests to guard against drowning at sea.

Peasants used pebbles in their home-made remedies. In Spain rubbing oneself with a pebble gathered from the beaches of San Lucar or Chipina on Good Friday was thought to be a certain cure for fevers.

The hero Olger Danske is said to be under a spell in a cave beneath the ground, like Barbarossa. He has a long, fair beard which winds a thousand times around the table where he sits. His beard breaks through the ground and stretches as far as the Sund. Sometimes it is stirred by the waves and shows on the surface. When that happens, strangers think it is seaweed, but sailors know it is Olger's beard.

The Friesians used to have pictures of seaweed on their shields to bring them victory.

In the Aleutians everyone used talismans, and it was believed that a warrior who went into battle wearing seaweed tied in certain magic knots could be certain of winning his battles.

In Scotland seaweed is used as a fertiliser. Early on New Year's Day farmers hurry to gather the first strands of seaweed from the beach. They take them home and put a little at each door and in each of their fields. They say this brings good luck.

Cities beneath the sea

In many places the sea constantly batters the shore. In the end its slow but ceaseless action wears away the hardest rocks, and the damage done by the waves is clearly evident, sometimes after only a few years. But if the sea breaks not on hard cliffs but on sand-dunes or low rocks, it can force its way through these flimsy barriers and flood fertile lands, particularly at the equinoctial tides.

In historical times there are many examples of flooding by the sea. In Brittany around the 8th century a high tide flooded the forest of Scissey and the surrounding countryside, completely changing the outline of the channel coast from the mouth of the Couesnon to the Bay of St. Brieuc. A second flood completed the work of destruction. In Holland the Zuyder Zee, the Haarlemmer Meer and many other inland seas owe their origin to comparatively recent disasters. Along nearly all the coastlines of the world one finds stories of towns or shores engulfed by the sea either in written histories or in oral traditions.

This evidence of the power of the sea has captured the imagination of all coast-dwellers, so that they see certain drastic and sudden natural phenomena as events only explicable as the intervention of gods.

From classical times onwards there have been traditions which tell of cities engulfed by the sea under strange and marvellous circumstances as punishment for the crimes of their inhabitants. When the Achaeans of a certain town slaughtered the suppliants who had taken refuge in the temple of Neptune, the god showed his anger by means of an earthquake which destroyed their city. It was said that the earthquake was accompanied by a tidal wave which flooded the town and all the surrounding countryside (Pausanias). Another town not far away suffered the same fate. Acording to Ovid passing sailors used to point out the ruins of its walls and towers shattered by the sea.

On the sea-board of France many legends are told about the destruction by the sea of wicked cities and the castles of tyrants.

The disappearance of the town of Is is well-known, and it is said that in the 16th century people testified that whilst fishing at low tide they had often seen the foundations of old walls in the place which bore its name.

The sailors of Tréguier believe that the city of Grallon was not in Douarnenez but in their vicinity. The inhabitants of Penvenan and its environs say that the town of Is was situated in the place where the lonely beach of Trestel is now. Some say that marks on one of the rocks were made by the shoes of the Devil's horse, others that they were made by those of King Grallon. Sometimes the bells of the vanished town can be heard from beneath the waves. Another local legend says that a great city once stood where the reffs of Triagos are now.

The fishermen of Cancale believe that when the sea is calm and clear the ruins of walls can be seen between the islands of Chausey and the Mont St. Michel. These are the remains of a vanished town about which a legend is told: in olden times the English Channel was not as wide as it is today, and to get to Jersey one only had to cross a stream. However, there was a bay on the coast near Granville. The king of this region built a dam across it, behind which he placed his castle. In the wall of the dam there was a gate which led into the castle itself, and the king guarded its key carefully. One of his daughters was married to a local nobleman who wanted to seize the castle for himself and dethrone his father-in-law. He persuaded his wife to take the key of the dam gate and let the sea drown both the king and castle. They had a boat made ready so that they could escape when the water rushed in. The king's daughter made her father drink a sleeping-draught, and at midnight she and her husband opened the gate to let the sea in. But the fury of the waves was so great that they drowned the nobleman and his wife and submerged all the land around.

At Erquy (Côtes-du-Nord) people say that there was once a great city, Nasado, whose inhabitants were vicious and depraved. The women's complexions were so pale that when they drank wine it could be seen passing down their throats. God was angered at the excesses of the people of this city and stirred up the sea, which drowned the place and all those who lived there.

At La Repentie near La Rochelle the following legend is told about the place-name. There was once a rich man living on that coast, who had a beautiful estate and several children. One day he captured a mermaid in his nets whilst out fishing with his wife. The mermaid begged them to set her free. The husband would have done so, but his wife insisted on keeping their strange catch. The mermaid threatened to make them repent of their decision, but despite all her tears and threats she was taken to the house of her captors. A little while afterwards the sea rushed up the shore and destroyed their house, sweeping away the husband and the children along with the mermaid. The unfortunate wife was thus left widowed, ruined and utterly repentant.

Cardigan Bay is said to have been pleasant countryside long ago, before it sank beneath the sea. Welsh sailors report seeing the ruins of ancient buildings beneath the waters. According to Girard of Barry, Irish fishermen of the 12th century believed they could see shining beneath the sea the ancient round towers of a sunken city. There are yet other underwater towns off Southern England. An author who mentions them also writes of Irish legends about towns beneath the waters, amongst others the town of Inclidon near the cliffs of Moher. Those who get a clear sight of Inclidon are sure to become rich.

Where once the towers and magnificent houses of the ancient town of Stavoren were swallowed by the sea, tall grass and wheat now grow. The town was drowned because of the wickedness and pride of its inhabitants.

The old folk of Zula say that when the people of Adulis on the Red Sea became vicious and depraved, one day the sea swept in over their heads and their temples, burying the streets under sand-banks.

On the island of Wollen people tell that on the morning of Easter Sunday, Vineta, with its bronze gates, siver bells and silver counters which the children played with in the streets, rises up to the surface again (Bull. de la Soc. d'Anth. 1872, 610, after Temme).

On Sundays on the Baltic coast one can still hear the bells of cities sunk beneath the sea.

A church on the Baltic coast, when being desecrated by wicked men, suddenly sank down into the sea. At night the men can be heard sobbing as they sing the Penitential Psalms, and when the sea is calm the light of the candles they burn before the altar can be seen through the water.

In the open sea off Madras there are reefs which the local people say are the remains of a submerged city.

This belief in towns threatened with destruction was once very strong in Brittany. Before the French Revolution a candle was kept constantly burning in the chapel of Notre-Dame de Guéodet. If it went out, Quimper would undergo the same fate as the town of Is and be flooded by a well next to the church. The candle was still kept burning in 1792.

One very ancient document mentions towns swallowed up by the waves. In a report dated 1881 an orientalist mentions a story found in Egyptian papyri which contains many adventures similar to those of Sindbad the Sailor. After being shipwrecked, the hero of the story lands on an enchanted island where a snake tells him that when he leaves the island, it will changed into water and disappear.

Clouds

The sea around our shores is not the only sea known to folklore. Other seas mentioned in the legends of arctic regions lie beneath the surface of the world in the bowels of the earth. Some tales see there a complete world which, like ours, has a sky, a sun and everything necessary for a universe in miniature.

The sky above us also has its seas high above the clouds, and there can sometimes be links between them and us.

In primitive Aryan traditions the sky and the sea constantly impinge on one another, and the Bible seems to indicate a time when the waters above the firmament were separated from those below. Around Tréguier old sailors believe that once upon a time the sea bathed the firmament but later withdrew from it.

The Celts believed in a sea in the sky and even thought it possible to travel to the limits of the world to reach a sea in the clouds. Sir Francis Drake was thought to have done exactly this, returning safe and sound.

Celtic legend asserts the existence of this sea in the clouds. "If our fore-fathers did not lie", say the peasants of the Vendée, "there are birds who know the way to the upper sea and carry messages to the blessed souls in

Paradise".

According to Arab folklore Allah created several skies and in each of them he placed angels, seas and ice-mountains. Beneath the throne of the seventh heaven is a sea which sustains the life of all living beings, for it channels much needed rain from one sky to another. In the sky above the earth is a sea filled with animals like those who live in the seas of our world, kept there by the power of Allah.

A Japanese legend tells that the ancestors of that nation came down from the skies in a boat. The Malays say that their forbears, too, arrived on earth in a great ship made by the Creator of the universe.

In the Middle Ages various facts were quoted in the support of this belief. Gervaise of Tilbury tells that a Bristol sailor departed for Ireland, leaving his wife and children at home. His ship was driven way off course to the furthest reaches of the sea. One day his knife fell overboard as he was washing it after a meal. At that precise moment his wife was sitting at home in Bristol with their children when the knife fell through the half-open window onto the table. She recognised it at once, and when her husband returned, they compared dates and found that the loss of his knife and its arrival at his house coincided exactly. "After this example", demands Gervaise, "how can anyone doubt that there is a sea above our earth, in the air or above it?"

The Eskimoes thought that in a certain place the sky hung so low that a man could touch it with the paddle of his kayak. The sky had two large openings through which the upper sea could be seen.

Gervaise of Tilbury wrote that people returning from church one stormy day saw a ship's anchor caught in a pile of stones, its cable coming down from the clouds. They saw it tighten as if a crew were hauling on it without success. Confused voices could be heard from the clouds, and a sailor climbed down the cable. The moment he set foot on the ground he died of suffocation, as if he had drowned. An hour later the ship's captain cut the cable, and the vessel began to move away.

In many countries folklore links clouds with the sea. The vast amount of rain delivered in cloudbursts was not seen as having any connection with evaporation from the ground, an idea which was unknown to simple, uneducated people. This is probably what made them think that the source of rain must be an "inexhaustible stream". Hence also the idea that a cloud is a sort of water-skin which sucks up liquid from the sea and sprinkles it over the earth.

Cypriots used to think that after a fall of rain the clouds came down to the sea to take in more water. When doing so they would swallow up everything that they came across, men, animals and even stones.

Clouds are sometimes described as if they were evil birds who could be fought by violent means. A Breton folk-tale tells of a voyage when the sky suddenly darkened and the sailors saw rapidly bearing down on them a cloud so dreadful to see that it struck terror into their hearts. The captain ordered the crew to shoot arrows at its center. This they all did, except for one who hit the side of the cloud, which burst, discharging such huge quantities of water onto the ship that it sank.

Stars

In classical times, before the compass was invented, when lighthouses were rare and the configuration of the land-masses was imperfectly known, stars played a vital part in navigation. The same was true during the Middle Ages. It is not surprising to read that according to Mahomet stars were created to adorn the sky, stone the Devil and to guide man in forests and at sea.

When seafarers of classical times were unable to catch sight of any stars they became distinctly worried. Apollonius describes the fear of the Argonauts when surprised by a dreadful darkness much dreaded by mariners (and called *Catoulas* or "fatal") in which the stars could not be seen.

Knowledge of the stars was one of the most highly-prized skills of a sailor. Manilius says that a good pilot must know the stars well, for the sky is the guide for all his navigation. There is also a Russian saying: "Ships sail by the stars".

When Europeans first made contact with the peoples of the Pacific, they found that observation of the stars was just as highly esteemed by them as by the mariners of ancient times, and for the same reasons. Aotoru, who was brought back to Europe by Bougainville, could name the majority of the stars pointed out to him by the ship's crew.

Many years ago the sailors of Trégor in Brittany had a strange theory about the origin of the stars. According to an old salt known as Lame Vincent, who had made many voyages to Newfoundland, old sailors said that the stars were huge diamonds left high-and-dry when the sea receded and ceased to wash over the heavens. He added that not all the water had disappeared, and that what remained formed a river flowing round the sky (this is probably the Milky Way or St. James's Way). In this river there were millions of stars slowly growing, like rocks in the sea.

This sailor had got to know an old Indian in Newfoundland who thought that the stars were snakes' eyes and that the celestial river was full of snakes of all sizes whose eyes and scales shone in the darkness.

In Irish folklore stars are believed to be cods' eyes. This idea of stars as eyes is very widespread, especially in New Zealand.

People of classical times noticed that at certain times stars seemed to disappear into the sea and concluded that, like the sun, they went there to bathe and take nourishment. In the *Odyssey* Homer says of one of the best-known stars: "The Bear, commonly known as the Chariot, turns in the same places as the Pleiades, the Hyades and mighty Orion and is the only one not to bathe in the ocean". Hesiod and several other Greeks authors testify to this belief, which was still held towards the end of the Roman period. Cicero writes: "The constellation of Boötes is the last to disappear beneath the sea when the day breaks." This ancient idea seems to have persisted in Greece: a Cretan folk-song tells of a place at the ends of the earth where the stars bathe.

According to Plutarch, Thales observed that the stars fed on the vapors of the sea. Cicero said that they fed on the vapors which the sun draws from land, sea and waters. According to Lucian the stars will one day be extinguished in the depths of the ocean.

Columella wrote: "The setting of certain stars foretells a storm. Often it is the cause."

Arab seafarers of the Middle Ages noticed that the state of the sea coincided with the movements of the stars. The Persian Gulf starts to get stormy when the sun enters the sign of Virgo. The waves grow rougher until the sun enters the sign of Pisces. They are most violent towards the end of Fall, when it is in Sagittarius and then grow calmer, becoming boisterous again when it returns to Virgo. The last waves appear towards the end of spring, when the sun is in Gemini. The Indian Ocean is very rough until the sun enters the sign of Virgo, which is the best time for sea-voyages. The greatest calms come when the sun is in Sagittarius.

Astrology had something to say about the sea: people used to look for favorable or adverse positions of the stars before going on board ship. In circumstances when a wrong decision would have been catastrophic, the Byzantine Emperor Manuel launched his entire fleet, the mainstay of his armed forces, at a time indicated by the stars.

Sicilian fishermen judge the time at sight by the position of the stars. They let down their nets when they rise, and when they catch no fish they wait for the appearance of a star which has not yet risen, for they say that fish, especially sardines, only move when the stars appear.

The ship of the sky is called Argo Navis to this very day. Others call it the ship of Osiris, whose pilot was Canopus. All ancient mythologies and astronomers agree the vessel is the one which goes by the name of Argo in poems celebrating the voyages of Jason. According to Orpheus it was built by Minerva and was the first ever to cross the sea.

Next to Argo Navis there are stars which represent the rocks on which it is wrecked.

Cicero writes: "Near the tail of Canis Major Argo Navis sails stern-first, facing the opposite way from all the other ships which plow the fields of Neptune. Like sailors bringing their ship stern-on to the shore when entering harbor, Argo sails poop-first across the immensity of the skies. From mast to stern there are no stars but between mast and stern there are some very brilliant ones. The rudder, picked out by a few minor stars, is to be found in the lower reaches of Canis Major."

This ship was placed in the heavens by Minerva to give confidence to sailors. Hyginus says that it is only marked by stars from stern to mast so that sailors should not be dismayed by damage to the foreparts of their own vessels.

Of the Pole Star an ancient author writes: "Except for sea-captains there are few amongst the general run of sailors who do not think that the star called Pole Star, Star of the Sea or North Star is named thus because it is in fact at the pole of the world, and that the whole universe turns on this star as if on a golden pivot. Indeed the Tartars call the Pole Star "Senesticol", which in their language means "Iron Nail".

In the Mediterranean it was also called the *Tramontana*, because sailors from Marseilles and Genoa used to see it above the lands which lie *tra monti* (on the other side of the mountains). Hence the French expression *perdre la Tramontane* (losing the Tramontana), which implies having no way of getting out of a jam, being lost like the pilots of old when they lost sight of the Pole Star, or not knowing which way to turn.

When the voyagers of the 15th century passed over the line and lost sight of the Pole Star, they were frightened. Columbus used to tell his crew that it was not because the compass needle had lost its power, but because the Pole Star had moved.

When French sailors say that the wind has veered *à l'étoile* (to the star) they mean to the north, as that is where the Pole Star is.

The Pole Star has sometimes been used in the imagery of popular poetry:
Por la estrellita del Norte
Se guian los marineros;
Yo me guio por tus ojos
Que parcecen dos luceros.
(Sailors are guided
By the Pole Star
As I am guided
By your eyes shining like two stars)
Eres la estrella del Norte
Que a los marineros guia
Desde que se hace de noche
Hasta que se hace de dia.
(You are the North Star
Which guides the sailors
From the fall of night
To the break of day)

Breton sailors say a shooting star "drowns itself in the sea". This belief dates back to classical times as can be seen from this quotation from Theocritus: "Suddenly he fell into the waters like those stars which come away from the firmament and plunge into the sea".

According to a curious belief current in the Middle Ages shooting stars are the half-digested food of white gulls.

Such stars also served as a portent. According to Seneca, mariners saw a large number of shooting stars as a sign of fine weather to come. Theophrastes writes: "If on a dark night one sees several shooting stars at the same time when there is a white cloud in the sky, there will be wind from the quarter where they fall. If they fall in different or opposite places there will be a storm."

Aristotle considered that comets foretell storms, strong winds and heavy rain. The comet that appeared during the consulate of Paterculus and Vopiscus made the words of Aristotle and Theophrastes come true: in its wake there were violent, ceaseless storms. This belief can be found in Homer: "Like a fatal comet leaving the blue sky at the command of Saturn's son, like its fiery mane which makes sailors and warriors grow pale with fear and feel sinister portents in their hearts".

In the 16th century it was widely believed that comets caused great disasters, even at sea.

At the beginning of the 18th century comets still inspired great fear in Norman sailors. At Assinie on the Gold Coast when a comet is seen all normal activities cease and all canoes are beached.

Like shooting stars, comets were said to plunge into the sea. The author of *Things Not Generally Known* writes that when he was a child, his nurse, who was born in Sussex, told him that she had seen the great comet of 1769 from the cliffs of Eastbourne. It had come down in the sea and plunged its fiery tail into the water without so much as a hiss.

The sun

In classical times people did not see the earth as a globe floating in space. When the sun rose it seemed to come up out of the sea, and when it set it seemed to disappear into the waves again. Hence the sea was thought to be its dwelling-place during the night.

According to the most ancient beliefs about the sun it plunges in the sea and extinguishes its fires in the cold waters.

This belief was held by the ancient Saxons, and people of classical times also thought the sun and the stars fell into the sea.

The Egyptians also had the idea that the sun passed through the sea at night. In the *Odyssey* the sun both begins and ends its journey there. In the *Iliad* it rises from the waves of the calm sea, and its brilliant light falls into the ocean at the end of the day. This belief persisted for a long time, even after the Romans reached the western limits of Europe. Florus tells us that Scipio only brought back his legions after seeing the sun plunge into the sea and bury its fires under the waters, a sight impossible to observe without fear of sacrilege and a feeling of religious horror. Statius relates that the sun unhitches his horses and washes his hair in the waters of the ocean. Later the Stoics thought that the sun drew its light from the sea and fed on its waters. According to Germanic folklore the sun washes during the night, which accounts for its shining face the next morning.

In Greece the sunset is called the "plunge of the sun". In Cyprus a similar expression is used.

Slav folklore says that at night the Sun-God takes a bath to purify himself and in the morning rises fresh and clean, with renewed brilliance. The sea is the mother of the sun, and during the night it sleeps in her arms.

Breton sailors that the sun sets in the sea to regain its strength and appear with renewed brightness the next morning.

The expression "the sun will set in the sea" is much used by sailors of the Channel coast. In Spain, where the same belief prevails, the sun is said to splash about at the bottom of the sea before rising on Midsummer Day.

In classical times Greek sailors, like everyone else, feared eclipses of the sun. When Pericles was commanding the Athenian fleet he saw that the master of his ship was badly scared by an eclipse of the sun, so he held up his cloak to shade out the sun and said: "Do you think that what I am doing is a bad omen? Of course not! Well, it is just as much an eclipse as the one you can see, except that the moon is much bigger than my cloak and shades the sun from many more people."

In Scotland fishermen feel in danger if they happen to put out their boats on a course opposite to the sun's. Orkney fishermen say that boats should sail like the sun, from left to right. This idea can be seen in a passage from a Saga in which an enchantress raises a tempest by describing circles in the opposite way to the sun's motion. In Scotland witches move around their cauldrons from right to left and ships must always head the same way as the sun. The fishermen of Macduff fold up their gear in the same direction as the sun's path.

The Jewish Midrash says the sun's course is like that of a ship with 365 ropes sailing from England or one with 356 ropes sailing from Alexandria (the solar and lunar years respectively).

The moon

Like the sun and stars, the moon was once thought to rise from the sea and return to it again. People of classical times believed this literally. One of the hymns attributed to Homer contains the words: "In the middle of the month the moon, having bathed its beautiful body in the sea each evening, harnesses its shining horses and urges them on eagerly."

The Greenlanders believe that the moon needs to seek its food on land and in the sea, where it catches dog-fish, its usual diet. When it is not in the sky it must be down below in the depths.

Simple-minded sailors believe that the moon is more useful than the sun, because it gives light in the darkness, whilst the sun shines during the day, when it is light anyway.

On the Channel coast people say that the moon governs the sea. The following legend makes this point: one day the sea smashed a fine ship on the rocks, and all its crew were drowned. The moon, angry with the sea, reproached it with having killed so many men and swallowed it.

Immediately all trade came to an end, for without water nobody could sail. One day a captain met the moon and said: "Ever since you have had the sea in your belly everyone has been dying of hunger, for all the ships are high-and-dry. You must take pity on the sailormen and put the sea back. They will be very pleased with such a favor from you."

So the moon said to the sea: "If you promise me one thing, I shall bring you out of my belly to the place you came from." "What is that?" asked the sea. "To be at my command always and to obey my orders." The sea agreed and was put back.

But some time later the sea fell out with its mistress, the moon. So the moon decided to swallow it again. The sea, once sweet, had by now become salt. The moon started to swallow the sea but found its taste so horrible that it spat it out.

Ever since then the moon has never again tried to swallow the sea. But the sea remains at the moon's command and must come and go as its mistress decides. Thus it is punished for having flooded a region rich in saltmines and turned salt.

Bartholomeus called the moon the servant and mistress of the sea. Alcuin called it the weather prophet. Two passages from Shakespeare make clear allusion to the idea of the sea's subjection to the moon. One is from the *The Winter's Tale:* "You may as well forbid the sea for to obey the moon as or by oath remove or counsel shake the fabric of his folly." The other comes from *Hamlet:* "The moist star upon whose influence Neptune's empire stands."

The effect of the moon on the tides is well known. English authors of the 16th century quoted by T. Harley make direct references to it and say that it exerts its influence over the seas and over all liquids.

In China its vital force governs water, which it is the reason why the tides are highest when the moon is at its brightest.

Eclipses of the moon were greatly feared by the sailors of classical times. During the Peloponnesian War the Athenians had made all their preparations and were about to set sail when the moon went into eclipse, being then at the full. Most of the Athenians were worried by this and asked the generals to put off the expedition. But Nicias, who always attached great importance to such things as portents, declared that all discussion on the matter would have to be postponed until the end of the eclipse, twenty-seven days by the priests' reckoning.

In China at eclipses of the moon people light up their houses and boats with lanterns and colored glass, strike gongs and make a deafening noise to scare away the monster which is trying to devour the moon. Sailors are the most enthusiastic helpers on this occasion and make more noise then everyone else.

Sea-mist

French sailors sometimes compare sea-mist to a sand-bank which bars their way or a curtain which hides the way ahead. In the 17th century Père Fournier called it "nature's curtain", and to this day one speaks of a curtain of mist."

In northern waters off Newfoundland and in the seas around Britain mists are sometimes so thick that they become a "sea-lung" of the kind mentioned by Pythias of Marseilles and classified in classical times amongst the elements, along with fire, earth, water and air.

In various forms mist is one of the greatest hazards to navigation. Sometimes it is so dense that the expression "lost in the mist" is far from being a figure of speech.

When there is a sea-swell, the people of Newfoundland say it "smells of mist". In Lower Brittany mist makes the sea rise. Around St. Malo it is regarded as a sign of a coming sea-swell.

Off the coast of New England fishermen use the word "fog-swell" to describe the swell of the sea which sometimes comes up during a mist, and they think the mist is the cause.

Sailors used to think mist had a supernatural cause, as in other matters they fear but cannot understand. In Brittany, where sailors think the sea is governed by the moon, they say that when the moon is angry with the sea it causes the mist as a punishment. In other places demons, goblins and even gods, sometimes visible but more often not, are the cause of fogs or use them as a screen behind which they do terrible things.

On the coast of Cornwall they say the *hooper* of Sennen Cove was a spirit which appeared in the form of a bank of fog. It spread over the whole bay and was so thick that visibility was nil. It was regarded as the kindly action of the spirit, which wanted to dissuade fishermen from venturing out into the open sea.

The mist was always followed by a violent storm at sea. One day a sceptical old fisherman ignored the warning, put to sea with several men and took with him a whip which he said he was going to use to thrash the spirit. He passed through the mist and out to sea. Then a great tempest blew up, and his boat disappeared for ever. Since then the hooper has rarely been seen.

Sir Walter Scott tells that when there is a mist in the North Sea, fishermen say they can make out the horns of the Kraken moving in its midst.

To blow away the fog or make it less dangerous, various magic devices were used in ancient times. Nowadays, however, coasts are well provided with buoys and beacons, and in certain spots there are bell buoys which ring with the motion of the sea and warn mariners of reefs or rocks. Big ships use a fog-horn to warn others of their approach.

Warning bells are not such a modern invention as one might suppose, in fact they have been in use since the Middle Ages.

In Scotland local folklore tells of a certain Abbot of Aberbrothock who placed a bell on a raft near a dangerous rock. When the sea was calm it made no sound at all, but when the waters grew stormy it began to sound a warning to sailors.

One day a pirate ship, to anger the Abbot, cut the ropes which which tied the bell to the raft. It fell to the bottom of the sea, ringing loudly, and the pirates made off. Some time later the pirate ship returned laden with plunder, was overtaken by a thick fog and wrecked on the very rock of Inchcape which now had no bell to give warning.

When in danger from evil spirits sailors have been known to use magic to scare them off. Sometimes they used a sword. During the voyage of the Argonauts they were suddenly wrapped in a dense fog. They prayed for the help of Apollo, who appeared, shot arrows into the fog and cleared it away. In the

Kalevala the hero Wainamoinen strikes the waters of the sea with his sword, and suddenly the surrounding fog lifts and disappears into the sky. Perhaps a faint memory of such things can still be seen in the expression "a fog you could cut with a knife".

Mirages, St. Elmo's fire and phosphorescence

The strange phenomenon of sea or coastal mirages is linked with mist. Indeed they are often seen before or after it.

Mirages look like the most diverse things, ships, castles, forests or towns. On Friday 15th August 1873 the inhabitants of Flushing suddenly saw an entire town rise up out of the sea. Through a light mist they could make out houses and trees.

A sea-captain gives this description of a mirage he once saw after a fog: "Before us was a long, rectangular mountain. One of its northern faces reflected the light with dazzling brilliance. Half-way up there was a deep line like a plinth right across it, seeming to make a division between two floors. Above this line there were evenly-spaced cavities like a symmetrical pattern of windows. Below it were other, larger cavities like porticos, columns and entablatures... We had neither a map nor a description of the place and no exact idea of the actual position of Monterey. This uncertainty must have been the cause of the error we now made under the influence of the optical illusion. We assumed that the mountain was the governor's residence, placed half-way up the hill. At its foot lay the town of Monterey. A few hours later we would be able to put into harbor and enjoy a good rest, or so we thought.

We immediately steered for the shore, but soon, as if by magic, the castle disappeared, the crosses and porticos turned into cracks and dreadful rock crevices, and the architectural masterpiece was just a vast ruin."

Mirages are doubtless the origins of illusory islands and land which recedes before one like a will-o'-the-wisp.

Tacitus lists amongst portents of disaster the mirage of a city seen, upside-down, on the waters of the Thames.

According to poems attributed to Orpheus, in classical times the origin of St. Elmo's fire was traced back to the voyages of the Argonauts. Diodorus Siculus relates that when the Argonauts were overtaken by a gale Orpheus prayed to the gods of Samothrace, and the wind immediately dropped. It is even said that two stars fell on the heads of Castor and Pollux, an event which astonished everyone and was taken as a sign that the gods were going to rescue them from danger. Hence, when seafarers were storm-tossed they used to offer up prayers to the gods of Samothrace and see Castor and Pollux themselves as two stars.

On the coast of Brittany St. Elmo's fire is thought to be lost souls begging a parent or friend for prayers or masses. Other sailors think that it is drowned men climbing aboard the ship they have sailed in to ask for prayers for their salvation. This belief is found on the Atlantic coast. According to stories told by American whalers the fire is the soul of a sailor who has died on board.

In Germany it is thought to be souls of the dead who are wandering because they have not received Christian burial and thus cannot find eternal rest.

Telonia is a kind of electricity which can be seen at the mast-head during storms. The Greeks saw it as birds of ill-omen which perch on the masts to destroy the ship and its crew.

Here are two folk-tales involving St. Elmo's fire.

Once there was a captain who found a shipwrecked man floating on the waves in a tiny, battered skiff. He picked the man up, looked after him and put him ashore. Now the shipwrecked man was St. Elmo, and when he stood safe and sound on land he asked the captain how much he owed for his rescue and care.

"Nothing", said the captain, "What I have done, I have done for the love of God and because that is the way one sailor ought to treat another. You say you are a saint. Saints work miracles, so work one for me to prove the truth of what you say."

"Since you do not want money," said St. Elmo, "I am going to show my gratitude by doing you a great favor. When a storm is near I shall send fire to warn you and all other sailors. If you see it at the masthead or at the yard-

138

arms, look out for bad weather."

At the same time St. Elmo wished the captain the greatest possible prosperity and went up to Heaven before the eyes of the entire crew.

The captain made a good voyage, thanks to the fire which gave him warnings of storms. Ever since that time St. Elmos fire has appeared to warm mariners of rough weather in the offing.

Once there lived in Calabria a hermit called Elmo. He begged for alms, and everybody gave him something. One day his brother died, leaving seven sons in dire poverty. St. Elmo took them into his care. From that time on those who had given him alms would do so no longer. St. Elmo was praying to God for help when there appeared before his cave a giant with a lantern in his hand. The giant said he had been sent by God to help him by means of the lantern. St. Elmo went down on his knees, amazed by this strange answer to his prayers. Now the giant was St. Christopher, who told him that the lantern would shine at sea on dark nights to help smugglers in danger of their lives. St. Elmo did as he was told and placed the lantern on a rock in the sea. Thereafter he always returned to his cave with a bag full of gifts, and his nephews grew up to live lives of happiness and contentment.

Elsewhere one reads that St. Elmo was a Sicilian bishop who fell ill during a storm. When he lay dying he promised sailors in distress that he would appear to them if the were going to be saved. After his death a light appeared at the mastheads of ships and was named after him.

According to an English author, St. Elmo was really St. Erasmus, who is represented in early pictures as having a torch on his head.

In classical times the presence of St. Elmo's fire was regarded as an evil portent if there was only one light: Pliny writes "Stars come down and settle on the yards and other parts of the ship with a singing sound as if made by a bird of passage. This kind of star is dangerous when there is only one. It causes the sinking of the ship and if it falls into the hull it causes fires."

English, American and German sailors believe that if the fire comes below the rigging it is a sign of bad weather. Dampier said that if it appeared on the rudder it was usually a sign of misfortune.

English folklore says that as long as St. Elmo's fire shines on the mast the ship is under protection of a demigod of the air, but if it comes lower there will be a gale or some other disaster whose magnitude can be judged from the downward distance of the fire.

In China the fire is taken as an evil omen. If it comes down, it is a good sign—a belief completely opposite to the European one.

German sailors think that the balls of bluish light are only seen on vessels which have lost a seaman in an accident.

During Columbus' second voyage his companions thought they saw St. Elmo on the topgallant mast with seven lighted candles at his feet—no doubt seven fires which the crew mistook for the saint. They began to sing hymns and say prayers in the belief that the appearance of St. Elmo marked the passing of the worst of the storm.

Arab sailors also regarded this electrical phenomenon as a sign that a storm was ending. Returning seafarers told of a shape like a shining bird appearing at the masthead, giving out so bright a light that it was painful to look at. Once it was seen, the sea grew calm and the storm abated. The light disappeared without anyone being able to say how it came and went, but it was a definite sign that danger had passed (after Masudi).

Italian mariners of the 15th and 16th centuries interpreted the appearance of St. Elmo's fire as a sign of divine favor.

Portuguese sailors also saw it as a portent of the end of the rough weather.

German, English and American sailors think that if the fire appears on the rigging it foretells good weather.

Phosphorescence in the sea goes by many names. Most of them allude to its making the water light up or burn.

Bretons say that the sea-god has a magnificent garden at the bottom of the sea where dwell the souls of drowned men. It is adorned with diamonds and precious stones which glitter in the darkness and make the sea look as if were on fire.

Another piece of folklore says that the phosphorescence is produced by an enormous fish which inhabits the sea-bed and makes war on the other fish. It is called the Devil of the Waters. To kill its enemies it spits fire from its mouth which makes the surface look as it were in flames.

In Pomerania people think that in the place where this phosphorescence appears there is a devil who rides around on a barrel of pitch. Scottish folklore interprets phosphorescence in the sea or in waves breaking on the rocks as the sign of a great storm to come.

On the Grand Banks of Newfoundland a red glow in the sea foretells fog or great heat.

In Roman times phosphorescence was considered an evil omen.

Waterspouts

Because of their amazing effects, sudden appearance and strange shapes, waterspouts were the phenomenon which to primitive peoples most strongly suggested powerful monsters. Poetry has succeded so well in keeping alive in our minds the ancient animistic view of nature that we have to make a great effort not to see waterspouts as giants or sea-monsters. To the Chinese, the waterspouts which they saw so frequently off their coasts were dragons rushing nimbly through the air, which is why they were called *tatsmaki* or "spouting dragons".

In Japan there is a widely held belief that typhoons are caused by the passing of the dreadful dragon Riu or Tatsu Maki. It is a fantastic god living in the sea and capable of changing into a hundred different shapes, including human. It is feared, and at its altars prayers are said to it. According to one author the Tatsu Maki is a huge dragon which haunts caves at the bottom of the sea. Sometimes it comes to the surface and shoots straight into the sky, causing the turbulence that we call a typhoon.

A waterspout made by a genie was seen by the sultan of Samarkand and the King of Tartary on one of their journeys. They heard a horrible noise coming from the sea and a terrifying scream which made them tremble. Then the sea opened and a black column rose up, which pursued a meandering path towards the shore. Out of the column stepped a genie in the shape of a huge giant.

Sicilian sailors describe waterspouts as clouds which melt onto ships. They suck up the sea-water, rise in the air, pause for a moment and then carry the water off elsewhere.

Breton seafarers say that waterspouts sweep all obstacles aside with their long, dragging tails. This is the explanation for the deaths of many missing at sea, for a man caught by a waterspout or whirlwind will certainly be hurled overboard. A ship caught in its toils is in danger of destruction.

In classical times sailors used to pour a libation of vinegar to dissipate an approaching whirlwind.

Later, prayers, cannon-fire and magic were used.

The latter measures were based on the belief that waterspouts, like certain clouds, concealed magicians or devils, so sailors waved knives or clashed swords to scare them off.

In the Middle Ages, according to the Chronicle of John of Brompton, seamen would shout and bang the sides of the ship to put the dragon to flight. For the same purpose the Chinese and Japanese strike gongs and beat drums.

On one of Columbus' voyages the sight of waterspouts terrified his crew so much that they depaired of repelling them by human means. They began to recite passages from the Gospel according to St. John. When the waterspout had passed by harmlessly, they attributed their survival to the power of Holy Writ.

The winds

Although many cosmogonies say that the wind is one of the primordial elements, according to some sailors' stories the winds did not always blow over the sea. They lived in a distant country and until some brave sailors went there to seek them out, vessels could only move with the help of tides and oars.

There was once a captain who was sent to the land where the winds lived to find them and make them blow over the seas. In those days, there were neither winds nor waves, and sailors had to row wherever they wanted to go, which was tiring work.

The captain landed alone on the shore of the country where the winds dwelt. He caught them, put them in tightly-closed sacks, took them back to his ship and placed them at the bottom of the hold. The sailors were not told what cargo they carried, and the captain ordered them not to meddle with it. But one day they were bored, having no work to do and one of them said to his friends, "I must open one of those sacks, to find out what cargo we are carrying. Once I know, I'll close the sack up again quickly, and the captain will never find out."

The sailor went down into the hold and opened one of the sacks. It was the sack where the south-west wind was kept. It immediately escaped and began to blow so hard that in the blink of an eye, the ship was blown clean into the air and smashed into a thousand pieces. The other sacks were broken open, and the seven winds escaped. They scattered over the seas and have blown there ever since.

This story brings to mind the winds shut up in a leather sack by Aeolus and given by him to Ulysses. The sack was opened by sailors whose curiosity cost them their lives. Is the legend a popular version of this passage of the *Odyssey*, or did Homer and the Breton story-teller have common folklore source? It is difficult to be certain. It can be taken for granted that the tradition is an ancient one, particularly if one accepts that the *Odyssey* is really a collection of legends to which Greek genius gave an immortal form.

In the Breton legends the winds are not described as creatures of flesh and blood, but rather as spirits which blow air, an aspect which agrees with the myth of Aeolus. Other stories from Upper Brittany depict the winds which were brought from their own country in order to blow over the sea as real and tangible persons.

There was once a company of ship-owners who had many ships, but since in those days there was no wind over the sea, the sailors grew tired of endless rowing. Not one of them was willing to go on board ship, and the beautiful vessels all stayed in the harbor.

The owners were so angered by this that they swore they would sell themselves to the Devil. One day a fine gentleman came up to one of them and asked, "What is making you so unhappy?" The owner told him that his men would not board the ships and row them. The man said, "They tell me that you would sell yourself to the Devil if you would find a way of getting your ships out of harbor. I am the Devil. If you will give me your soul, your ships will always move without any need for rowing." The owner was delighted. He took the Devil to his home, but instead of offering him his own soul, he offered him that of an old sailor, and the Devil who is not too particular, thought the deal a good one. So he told the ship-owner, "In the islands of the sea there live people whose breath is strong enough to blow a house down. These people are called Winds. Send one of your captains to find them. As soon as they are on the ocean, all ships will move without using oars." The Devil also told him where to find these islands, then he vanished, after telling the ship-owner that he would come and see him again when the Winds arrived.

The shipowner assembled his captains, and told them what had been said. One of them replied, "I will go and find the Winds, but only if after a year and a day you will give me the ship under my command."

146

The owner agreed, the captain got together this crew and set off taking with him the Devil, who had promised to go along. The voyage was a long one because the trip had to be rowed, and the crew were beginning to get restive when an island was sighted. They steered for it, and the captain and crew went on shore. The Devil stayed on board.

The captain went to see the Winds and he persuaded them to come on board by promising them to let them look over the ship. Whilst they were eating and drinking in his cabin, the ship left the island.

After a while one of the Winds came on deck and when he saw that they were on the open sea, he became frightened. He called his companions, and the North Wind, their leader, was no angry that he scared even the Devil, who left the ship.

However, the ship continued its voyage and since sails had been put up, on the Devil's advice, the breath of the Winds blew it along.

But the Winds were angry at having to travel over the sea against their wishes, so they swore that on the first coastline they reached they would blow so hard that the ship would broken into a thousand pieces. They kept their word: as soon as the coast of France was reached, they took a deep breath and in the twinkling of an eye the ship was blown onto the rocks and smashed.

The sailors managed to reach dry land. The Winds were left without a ship to take them back to their island and so stayed over the seas. As they have now forgotten their homeland they stay there for ever, and while the world lasts there will be ships under sail.

Another Breton story says that there was once a captain from Saint-Cast who left St. Malo to go to Newfoundland. Near Legeon he saw a man calling for help on a rock. The captain sent a boat for him, and the shipwrecked man was taken on board. The anchor was dropped so that the current would not take the ship onto the rocks. In those days there was no sea-wind, and ships had to follow the direction of the current. When the anchor was down the captain told his men to sleep whilst they waited for the tide to allow them to continue their voyage. He found himself alone with the shipwrecked man, who asked him where he was bound for.

"For Newfoundland", he replied.

"For Newfoundland? I don't think you will get there."

"I will get there in good time, and I hope to do well."

"I can bring you luck, but you will have to give up the idea of Newfoundland this time."

"What are you talking about?" cried the captain. "If I do not get to the fishing-grounds, what will become of my wife and children?"

"They will lose nothing by it, quite the contrary. Take me back to St. Malo and I will tell you my secret."

The captain had the anchor raised, and they returned to St. Malo. The shipwrecked man, who was in reality a saint, then asked him, "Have you heard of the winds, captain?"

"Yes, and I have even heard that the king would give his best ship to the man who could get them out over the sea."

"Exactly! If you listen to me, you will be the one who gets the king's best ship. Go to the land of the Winds and they will follow you back. But first I must tell you my secret. Although I was on the rock, I could easily have rescued myself if I had wanted to, for I am a saint and my name is St. Clement, but I wanted to see if you were kind-hearted. You helped me, so it is right that I should reward you. Bring your mouth close to mine." The captain obeyed, and the saint blew into his mouth and told him, "Ever since the Winds were first created I have been their master, and they obey me. When you find them you have only to blow and they will obey you as they obey me. You will make them board your ship, and when they are over the open sea you will get the king's ship."

The captain thanked the saint, who immediately vanished. He left for the land of the Winds and it was a long journey, because the tides were not always favorable and the sailors grew tired of non-stop rowing. At last they reached their destination. The captain left the ship and when he came to the Winds, he said to North Wind.

"Captain, you and your crew have been in this country for a long time now. I have been ordered to take you elsewhere and I have come to fetch you."

North Wind was unwilling to go with the captain and grew angry. He and his crew blew on the captain and tossed him about in the air as if he were a dead leaf. The captain then remembered the power given to him by St. Clement and blew back with all his might. Immediately the Winds calmed down, became as docile as sheep and followed the captain on board his ship.

The ship did not take long to return to France, because the Winds blew constantly on the sails. The ship sailed as well on the ebbtide as on the flood-tide, and the crew were pleased that they no longer had to row.

The captain disembarked the Winds and they scattered over the ocean, were they have been blowing ever since, and thanks to them, sailors no longer have to row in order to move their vessels.

The King of France was delighted to see the Winds were out over the seas, had the captain brought to him and gave him his finest ship. Soon afterwards the latter gave up sailing and stayed at St. Cast with his wife and children. In gratitude to St. Clement for the service he had done him, the captain had a statue of him placed in the parish church, where it is still to be found.

Stories of a time when the winds had not yet begun no blow are to be found in other legends.

According to a legend of the Algonquin Indians, eternal winter once reigned over the earth because warm winds never blew. One day a little animal called the fisher, helped by some of the beasts who were his friends, made a hole in the canopy of the heavens which led into the heavenly land, so that the warmth-bearing winds could come down and summer descend upon the earth. Then it opened the cage where the birds were imprisoned. The birds escaped and warm winds began to blow over the world.

The gods of the winds play an important part in the polytheism of all races. The winds themselves, and especially the four winds which blow from the four cardinal points, often take the name and shape of gods personified.

Aeolus was the chief of the winds, and was credited with power over them, but other gods, Jupiter, Neptune, Amphitrite, Minerva, Vulcan and even lesser gods were able to command them. In the *Odyssey*, Circe had power over them and granted Ulysses a favorable wind.

In Hindu mythology, Rudra, chief of the winds and of storms, ended up by becoming the god of destruction under the name of Siva.

In Scandinavian poetry Baldur is master of the winds; he rules the seas and fire. He is invoked at sea and when fishing.

A popular tradition in Russia makes the four winds the sons of the same mother; the ancient Russian *Lay of Igor* addresses the wind as if it were a noble, and the winds are called grandsons of Stribog, whose divine nature is indicated by the word *bog* (god).

The myth of the four winds is very popular in the folklore of the American Indians. The west wind is the father of the winds and his name is Mudjekeewes. Wabun is the east wind, Shawondasee the south wind, Kabibonokka the north wind. One of the winds who is not part of this mysterious quartet is Manabozho, the north-west-wind, who in folklore is understandably represented as the illegitimate son of the father of the winds. Man naturally thinks of the world as a square with the wind in the four corners.

In the Pacific the myth of the winds is still current. The system of the many gods who rule them is very complicated. Ellis says that the principal gods of the winds of Polynesia are Veromatautoru and Tairibu, brother and sister of the children of Taaroa. They live near the great rock on which the world rests. It is supposed that hurricanes and tempests are enclosed with them and that they release them to punish those who neglect to worship the gods.

The ancients had a symbolic system which gave certain signs of the zodiac to each wind and also attributed winds to each sign. Here is an interesting excerpt from an ancient chronicler on this subject.

The signs of the zodiac were divided in threes amongst the winds which blew from the four cardinal points: the three fire signs, Aries, Leo and Sagittarius went to Aquila, the north wind; Taurus, Virgo and Capricorn, the three earth signs, to Auster, the south wind; Gemini, Libra and Aquarius, the air signs, to Aphetiotes or Subsolanus. The water signs, Cancer, Scorpio and Pisces were assigned to the African wind blowing from Libya.

Not only were the four sets of signs divided amongst the four winds but a wind was assigned to each sign. The wind Africus was assigned to Aries, Circius to Taurus, Aquila to Gemini, Septentrionus to Cancer, Thrascias to Leo, Agestes to Virgo, Zephyrus to Libra, Africus to Scorpio, Auster and Africus to Sagittarius, Auster to Capricorn, Norus to Aquarius and Evrus to Pisces.

In his *Travailleurs de la mer,* Victor Hugo makes the remark that when one lives close to the sea, it is difficult not to look upon the winds as a person and the rocks as individual people.

In Sicily because of the strength of the wind, the people say it is of the masculine gender; this relates to Seneca's idea. The Egyptian said that the wind was masculine air, whilst still air was feminine.

In a Sicilian story there is a meeting of Winds, Water and Honor, who discuss their relative merits. Wind tells them how he works windmills, that without him ships would not be able to move, and that when he has nothing to do he plays with clouds or trees on the peaks of the highest mountains. The three agree to give each other a signal so that they can meet again, and Wind says that ordinarily he can be found on the peak of Mt. Gibel, palying with clouds and smoke.

Worship of the winds was very common in classical times. Their shrines could be seen in many places on shores, capes or mountains.

Phoenicians put up columns in honor of the elements, one of them being specially dedicated to the air and winds. The ancient Persians offered up sacrifices to them. The people of Megalopolis made an annual sacrifice to Boreas and planted a grove sacred to him.

In the *Iliad* Achilles pours libations to the winds Zephyrus and Boreas and promises them sacrificial victims if they fan the flames of Patroclus' pyre. Herodotus writes that Menelas sacrificed two Egyptian children to the winds. The Greeks sacrificed to Boreas before descending on the Persian fleet at Magnesia, and the same was done before the battle of Artemisium.

The Gauls also honored the winds. Although Circius blew their dwellings down, they still offered him thanks for keeping the sky clean. While in Gaul Augustus vowed to build a temple to Circius, and did so, according to Seneca.

Roman generals, when facing danger, prayed to the winds, amongst other deities. Sometimes they poured libations to them into the sea.

The Estonians used to pray to Tuule Ema, mother of the winds, and when a gale was blowing used to say "The mother of the winds is groaning, who knows how many other mothers will groan in their turn?"

Grimm quotes an old saga in which Scandinavian seafarers offer three barrels of ale to Freya to have good winds for their voyage to Sweden, and to Thor or Odin for good winds to Iceland.

Once when a junk was held up by contrary winds, the crew threw a barrel of wine and some pieces of copper into the sea to appease Kompira, the god of the elements.

The Fijians pour a libation of khava and oil, saying, "Be kind to us, gods, and send us a favorable wind." In Brazil the natives had a similar custom in the 16th century.

In Cornish folklore the roaring of the wind is called "the cry from the northern abyss", after one Tregeagle, who sold himself to the Devil and was condemned ever after to clean out the Dosmary Pool. Whilst carrying sand he dropped some and thus caused a sandbank in the harbor. For that reason the winds are said to be the roaring of Tregeagle.

In French slang the wind is called *le gris* (literally "grey") or *le brisant* (derived from *brise* = breeze or *briser* = to break, the latter a possible tribute to its destructive powers).

English sailors call certain gusts of wind "sneezers". On the coast of America a north-westerly gale is known as a "sweeper of the sky".

Proverbs (3)

No es en mano del piloto que dexe el viento su soplo (Spanish: The pilot cannot stop the wind blowing).

Sail, quoth the king; hold, said the wind (English).

Sail quo' the king, Haud quo' the wind (Scottish).

El viento es el viento (Spanish: The wind is the wind).

On ne peut pas empêcher le vent de venter (French: You cannot prevent the wind blowing).

Barquan edo oncian enbarquatcendena estu bely dembora naihiduen becala. (He who embarks in a boat or ship doesn't always have the wind where he wants it).

Qui est sur la mer ne fait pas du vent ce qu'il veut (French: He who goes to sea does not do as he pleases with the wind).

Ilvo der segler paa Vandet, haver ikke Verwit i Haanden. Dic op de zee is heeft de wind niet in zijn handen (Danish and Dutch respectively: A seafarer does not have the wind in the palm of his hand).

Qui maria sulcant, ventum in manibus non habent (Latin: Those who plow the waves do not hold the wind in their hands).

Man kand ey segle hvor hen man vilde' men hvor Vinden bloeser (Danish:

You can't sail where you want but where the wind blows).

Plogja of inkje saa, fria og inkje faa, og sigla med ingen Vind: er tri gagnelause Ting (Plowing without having sown, giving without receiving,- setting sail without a wind, these are three futile things).

A grand vent petite voile, Hard windt klein zeil (Breton and Dutch respectively: In a great wind you need a small sail).

Il faut tendre la voile selon le vent ; Bisogna voltar la vela secondo il vento (French and Italian respectively: You must rig your sail according to the wind).

Door wind en stroom is goed stuuren (Dutch: Wind and current behind you make good sailing).

Vento potente, fote la corente (Venetian: A strong wind overcomes the current).

Facile est dare vela secundis (Latin: It is easy to sail with the wind).

Avoir le vent en poupe ; Avere il vento in poppa (French and Italian respectively: To have the wind aft).

Mon naplis éna divent dériére (Mauritian Creole: I haven't got the wind aft).

Vent arrière fait la belle mer (Breton: Wind aft makes a good sea).

Ognun sa navigare quando e buon vento ; Ognunu sa navicari cu bon ventu; A bentu in favore ognunu ischit navigare; Ognun sa navigare col buon vento (Italian, Sicilian, Sardinian and Tuscan respectively: Anyone can sail with a good wind).

Quam bene navigant quos fortuna dirigit! (Latin, Seneca: How well they sail who have Luck at the helm!).

Il n'y a pas de mauvais pilote quand le vent est bon (French: When the wind is good there's no such thing as a bad sailor).

Quand il n'y a point de vent, chacun sait naviguer (French: When there is no wind one man sails as well as the next).

Godt at sidde ved styret i stille Vand; i stille Veyr ere alde gode So-Moend (Danish: It is good to be at the helm when the wind is mild; in a calm everyone is a good sailor).

Seil, mens Vinden bloeser; Bören bier efter Ingen (Danish: Sail while the wind is blowing, for it waits for nobody).

Bören bier ester ingen. Seyl dersor n aar Vinden bloeser (Danish: The wind waits for no man, so sail while it is in your favor).

Mentri hai bon ventu, navica ; Men moel zeilen terwijl de wind dient (Sicilian and Dutch respectively: Sail while you have a good wind).

154

D'er inkje kvar Dag, Byren blaes (Norwegian: A good wind doesn't blow every day).

As the wind blaws seek your beild ("shelter"). (Scottish).

He that will not sail till he have a full fair wind, will lose many a voyage. (English.)

To set up his sail to every wind. (English, meaning "to be rash").

It's an ill wind that blows nobody any good (English).

De wind is nooit zoo slecht, of hij brengt iemancl vordeel an (Dutch: There is no wind as bad as the one which favors nobody).

Whichever way the wind blows, it must be against somebody (Norwegian).

No wind can equally serve the passengers (English).

To a crazy ship every wind is contrary (English).

Enhver Vind et loe skib imod (Danish: Any wind is contrary for a leaking ship).

The wind keeps not always the same quarter (English).

Ventus neque manere sinit neque navigare (Latin, Erasmus: This wind will allow a man neither to stay or go).

De duer ey at segle i ugiort Veder. Godt at segle med god Vind (Danish: It is not pleasant to sail in changeable weather. Sailing with a good wind in your favor is a real joy!).

A moderate wind is the best thing (Norwegian).

Aicia eta emastea eta fortuna cambiatcequo erraz dire hillaguyra becala (Basque: Wind, women and luck are as changeable as the moon).

Tempo, vento, signor, donna, fortuna.
Voltan e tornan come fa la luna.
(Italian: Weather, wind, lord, woman and fortune
change and turn like the moon).

Fimmina e ventu
Cancia ogni mumentu
(Sicilian: Women and wind change in a moment.)

La donna, la ventu et la vintura pocu dura (Sicilian: Women, wind and luck don't last long).

Mujer, viento y ventura presto se muda, Molher, vento et ventura asinha se muda (Spanish and Portuguese respectively: Women, wind and luck soon change).

A puff of wind and popular praise weigh alike (English).

Amigo del buen tiempo mudará con el viento (Spanish: A fairweather friend will change with the wind).

155

Amici de bonazza, inte le burasche i te nega (Venetian: A fairweather friend will desert you in a squall).

The prosperity of the shipowner is at the mercy of the wind (Tamil).

What the wind brings, the wind takes away (Iranian).

Gros vent, grosse mer, petit vent, petite mer (French: A rough wind makes a rough sea, a moderate wind makes a moderate sea).

Partir les vents et les mers : partager les dangers (French: He who parts wind and sea must share their dangers).

When wind and sea conflict, that's the time when we suffer most, said the ship (Arab).

Cásate vento
E amansarai.
(Spanish: Marry, o wind, and you shall sleep.)

The wind blows when sailors don't want it to (Arab).

Fancy flees afore the wind (Scottish).

Can any man seize the wind and put it in a vase? (Tamil).

He catches the wind in a net (Arab, meaning: he does something useless).

In ventum jactare brachia (Latin, Seneca: To fence with the wind).

He seizes the wind in his hand (Iranian, meaning: He cannot hold on to anything).

Puff not against the wind (English).

He that spits in the wind spits in his ain (own) face (Scottish).

He who spits in the wind soils his own face (Turkish).

If a man spits in the wind his spittle will land on his own face (Tamil).

Parlare al vento (Italian; To speak to the wind ; meaning: to be unheard).

A fool eats the wind (Ragusan).

Buy the clouds and sell the wind (Annamese).

In the following sayings or proverbs the wind is generally used in a figurative sense:

When glad to see someone, people used to say "What wind blew you hither?" and in French "*Quel bon vent vous amène!*".

In French *Arriver droit vent en arrière* (literally "to arrive with the wind behind one") means to arrive with one's hands in one's pockets and the rolling gait peculiar to sailors.

Expressions like "to sniff the wind", "to see which way the wind is blowing" are borrowed from life at sea.

The changeable wind of fortune drives us now onto the reefs of a stormy sea, now into a calm haven (Pindar).

Vent au visage rend un homme sage (French: Wind on his face makes a man wise).

By wind or water the wind is ever in my face (English).

Guess what one smells but never sees. Answer: the wind (Breton).

What is the thing without feet or legs that makes war? Answer: the wind (Russian).

The wind rose

The wind rose has thirty-two different points, but this arrangement is relatively modern, and the thirty-two winds do not all occur in proverbs, beliefs and superstitions. One must distinguish between those winds which are known to science and those which are pure folklore.

Certain winds are periodic, such as the Etesian and trade winds. According to Seneca sailors described the Etesian winds as sleepy and lazy, as, according to Gallion, they are late risers in the morning and never show themselves until the more forceful winds have died away. Cicero said that seafarers called them sleepy because they dropped during the night.

In classical times the trade winds were largely unknown. Of all the marvels discovered by the Spanish and Portuguese explorers on their voyages none amazed them more than these breezes constantly blowing from the same quarter. They were almost terrified by the constancy of the winds blowing steadily towards the Equator and never back to their homelands. Columbus' companions thought the winds were under a spell cast by the Devil, and they asked fearfully whether these airs might not carry them to some abyss at the edge of the world. However, mariners soon became familiar with the calm regions in the zone of the trade winds. Spanish sailors called this tropical part of the Atlantic "el golfo de las Damas" because even a girl could have steered a ship under those conditions. According to Varenius sailors leaving Acapulco were able to go to sleep and forget about the helm, certain that the wind would take them through the calm Pacific to the Philippines.

In Arabic *mussim* or *moussin* means a "change" or "season", and in effect these regularly periodic winds divide the year into two distinct parts. They are known as *moussons* in French and "trade winds" in English.

A belief mentioned in Shakespeare's *Hamlet* ascribes power over the mentally ill to certain winds: "I am but mad north-north-west: when the wind is southerly I know a hawk from a handsaw".

In sailors' tales in which the winds are personified, the north wind is their captain.

One day North Wind, captain of all the winds, had sent his crew to blow all over the world and in time they became discontented, for they had been blowing non-stop for years. They asked their captain for a few day's leave, but he refused.

"If this swine North Wind stays in command he'll kill us off in no time, for this constant blowing will ruin our lungs. We must mutiny and slit his fat belly!".

"Yes, yes", cried the seven winds "he must die!".

So they set off for his castle. South Wind said: "There you are, you villain! We'll soon be dead of exhaustion. You lead us a dog's life while you lounge about at home. With all this walking and blowing we're worn out, and I've got an arrow-wound in my leg just because I roughed up someone's garden. You shall pay for that!"

He made a sign to his shipmates and they all rushed at North Wind to kill him. But North Wind blew at them with all his might, sending them spinning into the air and rolling along the ground. That day they simply couldn't get their hands on him.

After they had rested they tried again the next day, and this time it was North Wind who was sent spinning into the air and rolling along the ground. He was scared and called for help, but nobody heard him. Just when his crew were going to slit his throat there was a great sound of drums and clash of arms: it was the king of France returning with his army from the wars. North Wind begged him for help and rushed to his side. But the seven winds began to blow so hard at the king's army that his soldiers were knocked flat on the ground and trees uprooted.

When they were out of breath the king of France mustered his men as

160

best he could and ordered them to open fire on the seven winds. The soldiers loaded and fired their muskets. The winds had never heard such a terrible noise. They stopped blowing and asked their captain's pardon, promising to obey him in all things in future.

North Wind was delighted. He invited the king and his soldiers into his castle and asked whether they had won their wars. "The war is not over yet," replied the king, "tomorrow is the final and decisive day." "Who are you fighting against?" "The Spaniards. They have won one battle and lost one. If they are victorious tomorrow all is lost", said the king. North Wind asked him to come back the next day and promised to join his side with all his crew.

The next day the king of France called on North Wind and his shipmates, gave them eight fine Norman horses and offered them weapons.

The eight winds accepted the horses but refused the arms, saying that they would get in the way.

They mounted and rode off with the king's army to where the enemy was drawn up in battle array. When the trumpets sounded for battle the winds blew at the Spaniards. These were sent flying into the air like chaff and thought the Devil had enlisted with the French. The king of Spain sued for peace, and when the winds had stopped blowing the Spanish soldiers fell back on the ground. But they were all dead, for the winds had stopped their breathing.

The king of France demanded and got the throne of Spain for his son as his terms for peace. This story was told in 1882 by François Marquer of St. Cast, cabin-boy.

In Scotland when the wind blows from south to south-west and clouds appear in the north-west, people fear a sudden squall. Fishing boats at sea run for shelter at top speed.

When the winds blow from the south and drive massive clouds before them, they say that the Earl of Moray will soon pay his debts to the Earl of Mar, meaning that the wind will soon veer to the north and bring changeable weather. The east-wind is known in the Mediterranean as the Greek wind or Levantas— *Vent grec, ploja au bec* (South wind, rain in its mouth).

In Asturias they say the west wind purifies the atmosphere.

Another proverb says *Vientu de cain, amor de bruxes* (The west wind is the sorcerer's delight).

In Scotland the wind which blows from the north-west and veers north in the evening is known as "the wife it gangs out at even".

The north-west wind is known in Upper Brittany as "Norouas" and in Lower

Brittany as *Awel fall* (Bad Wind). In the South of France they call it *Mistrau* or *Maistrau* (Nice), *Mistral* and *Magistrau* (Languedoc). It also bears the names *maestral* (Spain), *maestrale* (Italy) and *magister* (Low Latin). To Provence and the neighboring regions it is in fact the master wind. The north-west wind is nicknamed "broom of the heavens" by seafarers, as it sweeps the sky clear of clouds.

The Bora is the name given to the north-easter lies which blow in the Black Sea and also in the Gulf of Venice. The sayings about the Bora are much like those about the Mistral. In several parts of England north-westerly gales are known as "cats' eyes".

Folklore has given the north-west the title "master." In classical times, according to Strabo, it was known as *melamboreas*, overturned rocks and blew men off their chariots. When it arrived on the coast of North Africa, this "black breeze" hurls itself violently against the steep mountains of Algeria. It also has the sinister name "the Majorcan Shipright" because it smashes up ships and casts their wreckage up on the shore.

In the South of France the Mistral is also known as *Mistrau a derraba lo co dis ase* ("wind to blow a donkey's tail off").

Veu dou marin, quand boufo lou Mistrau (Woe to the sailor when the Mistral blows).

Quand le Mistraou bouffe, le diable est en Provence (When the Mistral blows the Devil is in Provence).

Se coumenco de jour.

Duro tré jour.

(If it starts during the daytime it will last three days).

Lou Maistrau couma trouva, laissa. (The Mistral leaves the weather as it finds it.)

That saying from the town of Nice has its exact counterpart in one from Venice: *La Bora, como la trova, la lassa.*

In Venice they also say *Maistrale duro, Siroco in culo.* (When the Mistral blows hard, it has the Siroco behind it.)

Lou Mistrau fai l'acoulado

Au soùleu de la valdo. (The Mistral drops at sunset and slackens towards high water.)

There is piece of folklore verse from Upper Brittany which goes like this:

> The sea is in a rage,
>
> Take care, you sailors.
>
> It blows from the north-west,

Look to the mast and sails,
For if the ship goes down
We shall be drown for sure.

West wind north about never haughs (blows) lang out (Scottish).

North-westerlies eat up a storm (Breton).

In Brittany the south wind is known as *Surouas* or *Suroît*. They say "The south-westerly is the sailor's carrier", and "wet as a south-westerly".

If the south-west wind does not stiffen after a squall, Bretons say there will be *malice* (spite) in the weather for several days.

Foretelling the weather

Sailors and fishermen, who always have the sky and the sea before their eyes and spend most of their lives on the waves, have always had a good deal of scope for observing the phenomenon all around them, thinking about apparent coincidences and making deductions about what they have seen. Thus a kind of empirical science arose which some rightly claim can predict the future weather and wind patterns by interpreting certain signs.

Before the compass and barometer were discovered, when the currents and the sea were little understood and there were no devices to transmit signals from one continent to another, this kind of science, this folklore guide to weather, was handed down carefully from generation to generation.

A passage from *Le jouvencel introduit aux armes*, written in the 16th century, advises youths to study meteors and the sea: "Those who wish to go to sea... must know the signs which foretell what is going to happen at sea and which appear by the light of the sun and the moon, such as winds, birds and fish." This advice had already been given by Vegetius.

To those who live by the water, the sea, like a person or animal, smells of the weather to come and predicts it by a particular sound, often called "song" of "moan". In Père Fournier's *Hydrographie*, written in the 17th century, there are axioms which define the views held at that time: "When the sea makes an unusual noise and the waves leave long patterns of sand on the beach, it is a sign of rain. If the noise of the sea carries far, even though the weather is calm at the time, there will soon be a storm."

In Brittany, when the sea roars into the beaches and against the cliffs, people say it "brays like a donkey". When people want to predict the weather or wind, they walk along the coast and examine the sea at each high tide. As the sea always makes a special sound in one place or another, they can tell what the weather will be like according to where the sound comes from. Some fishermen can predict the weather a week in advance using this method.

A proverb from Finistere also testifies to this belief:

Pa grosmolo ar mor,

Paourik, sarrit ho tor.

(When the sea growls dully, shut your doors, poor people.)

In England the term "calling of the sea" is used for a kind of groaning noise made by the sea. If it is very distinct, it is taken as a sign of bad weather.

On the shores of the Moray Firth in Scotland fishermen term it the "song of the sea". If it comes from the east, the wind will soon blow from the east or south-east. If a "long song" comes from the Bar of Banff, the wind will be from the east.

The appearance of the sea was also used for making predictions "When you see thick foam scattered over the sea, or little tufts of foam forming, it is the sign of a long, severe storm. The same applies when you observe the sea getting up suddenly."

Changes in the color of the sea was also said to predict the weather to come. Homer's *Iliad* (Book XIV) describes exactly this belief: "Even as the vast sea, fealing the approach of a storm, darkens its silent waves and waits calmly for the violent breath sent by Zeus..."

It reoccurs in the 17th century: "If the sea looks bluer than usual it is a sign of wind to come from the south; if the blue verges on black, the wind will come from the north; if in rough weather the sea suddenly grows calm, the wind will change, and often the new wind will be stronger than the previous one."

In the Mediterranean a reddening or swelling of the sea foretells rough weather.

La marino roujo

Auro pluico boujo.

(If the sea is red there will be wind or rain)

Quand la marino gounfle et que la tremountano boufo, taias de soupo, que lou bouioun mancara pas (When the sea gets up and the north wind blows, get your ingredients ready, the soup will not take long to boil).

Mari biancu, Sciroccu 'n campu (When the sea is white the Sirocco will blow over the plain).

Sailors thought that fish had a sort of instinct which enabled them to predict the weather, and that their behavior gives reliable clues about future weather. They studied fish closely, particularly the varieties which seemed to be particularly prescient.

In Brittany they say that fish bite well two or three days before the onset of rough weather, but will not touch bait on the day when the storm is due. They also believe that when big fish move about on the surface there will soon be a strong wind.

A proverb from Sicily agrees with this view: *Malu signu, quannu lu pisci di mare addiventa pisci di ciumi* (It is a bad sign when the fish of the sea appear on the surface).

Merk af Marsvin blesende Storm. (Danish: When the porpoises blow it is the sign of a storm).

According to an English author dolphins or porpoises playing in the sea foretell a storm. For this reason sailors see them as an evil portent. This belief also occurs in Ravenscroft's *Canterbury Guest:*

My heart begins to leap and
Play like a porpoise before a storm.

Other evidence for the currency of this belief can be found in Captain Cook and Shakespeare.

On the Charente people say it is a sign of rough weather when porpoises come close to the banks and rise out of the water after mullet.

In Scotland, if they turn over and over in the sea, sailors say that a breeze will spring up.

In France, Scotland and Germany seafarers believe that dolphins always swim to the side where the wind is to come from, and that they are swimming to meet it. This idea is also to be found in Bernardin de St. Pierre's *Voyage à l'île de France.*

Bretons take a different view of these signs. They think that when a dolphin leaps out of the sea it means fair weather, when he hardly emerges from the water and then submerges slowly, it is a sign of foul weather.

In the South Seas whalers say that whales grow restless when a storm is approaching.

Old fishermen believe that a leaping whale means a gale. The higher the

167

leap, the worse the gale will be.

American fishermen think that if whales swim around blowing, rough weather can be expected.

Marine life living alone the shore is just as sensitive to changes of weather as are the fish.

"When shellfish cling tightly to rocks or crabs seize stones in their claws or bury themselves in the sand, it is a sign of rain and storm." The people of the coast of Asturias say that when the lobsters leap, it is a prediction of foul weather.

Basset writes that many shellfish ballast themselves with sand when they know a gale is in the offing.

Plutarch believed that a cuttlefish on the surface, was the sign of a storm, a view still shared by some English sailors.

On the coast of Brittany people think that the wind never blows hard without a warning from the birds. Magpies lead the way, being noiser than usual; swallows swoop at one another, keeping aside from the rest; pigeons chase each other, flapping their wings loudly; geese flap their wings and cackle; stone-chats skim over the ground and seagulls flap their wings above the houses.

In Scotland, when sea-birds move inland making a great deal of noise, people regard it as a sign of an approaching gale.

In Brittany the flight of seagulls inland is seen as a prediction of rain or rough weather. The same belief applies in England, where they say

> "When sea-birds fly to land
> A storm is at hand"

and

> "Seagull, seagull, sit on the sand
> It's never good weather when you're on the land".

Cicero wrote of the seabirds' ability to foretell the weather: "When the white seagull warns us of the horrors of an approaching tempest, it rises above the waves and utters sharp, broken cries. Sometimes the carrion crow is also seen flying down to the beach to dip its head in the waves."

By their cries seagulls tell mariners of nearby shoals and approaching storms, and their predictions are more reliable than those of old salts. Disaster falls on those who kill them. They are cursed by the dying birds, whose malediction is not slow to take effect. It is said that the morning before the *Republican* was wrecked, its captain had killed some gulls flying over his quarterdeck.

168

Of all seabirds the petrel *(Procellaria pelagica L.)* is the foremost in foretelling foul weather, in several parts of the world his name implies this. In Picardie and Finistère it is called the "storm-bird", because it gives warning by flying low over the water and settling on ships. In England it is known as "storm-finch" and "stormy petrel". In Dutch a similar term, *Storm-valuw*, is used. Its other name is "devil-bird".

When Danish sailors see petrels flocking together in the ship's wake in a calm sea, they feel sure that a gale is coming, and their predictions are never ill-founded.

Other folklore speaks of the seabird *goylir* appearing before storms blew up. The Spaniards call it *malefigo* or "bird of evil".

The birds called by the Portuguese *almas perdidas* (lost souls) are always a sign of stormy weather.

The little stone-chats known as *satanas*, which follow ships, are also a storm-warning.

An ancient ballad speaks of curlews as the "seven whistlers" and says that their song at night tells that rough weather is coming.

In England the cuckoo's call predicts an equinoctial gale.

Other birds foretell tempests by their song. A cock-crow is thought by sailors to be the sign of a squall.

Seafarers took the swan as a portent of good weather, because, according to Emilius of Verona, it never dives beneath the waves and can ride out the worst gales.

An ancient belief, still found in the 18th century, held that kingfishers had the power of making storms die down and of predicting bad weather. Sailors used to think that if you hung this bird up by its beak it would immediately face the wind.

Spaniards see a sign of fine weather when gulls settle on the waves.

The Maoris of New Zealand say that the kohoperoa (a kind of cuckoo) stops singing when the wind is about to veer the south and only begins again when it springs up in the west or north again.

When albatrosses are hungry, it is a sign of fair weather.

In Upper Brittany, when seabirds stay out at sea, people say good weather is coming.

On the Breton coast very storm is foretold by signs given by animals. The cats sharpen their claws, pigs grunt, scatter their litter and move it around, sheep behave in a crazy way and butt one another.

In the Shetland Islands they say that if a cat looks at the clouds, it is a sign of wind to come; but if it sleeps with its head on its paws, it is a sign of calm weather. To know which way the wind will blow, you must notice which way a cat looks when it scratches the ground.

In Pomerania, they believe that in calm weather, when a cat lifts its head and sniffs, the wind will soon blow from the direction its head was pointing in.

Pigs have very small eyes, but in England some people believe that they are very good at predicting wind and rain, hence the expression "pigs seeing the wind".

Raising the wind

Sailors hate a calm. It delays their landfall and often precedes foul weather.

Around Tréguier they say, "When calm weather comes, nature is thinking" and "In calm weather the winds take counsel among themselves".

English mariners jokingly call a flat calm "an Irishman's hurricane". They also use this term for a wind which blows from all quarters.

In certain periods in the remote past, it is said, the sea was dead calm and the people of ancient times enjoyed "halcyon days" (the term "halcyon" refers sometimes to a fabled bird, sometimes to a kingfisher). This idea has provided many poets with a source of inspiration:

Willford, in his *Secrets of Nature* writes that the kingfisher when hatching his young in his floating nest forty days before the winter solstice, enjoys calm, tranquil weather, as has been observed on the coast of Sicily, which is the source of the phrase "halcyon days".

A parallel legend can be found in India: near Serendib there is a bird which hatches its brood on the sea-shore. Whilst it is doing this the winds stop blowing for forty days.

As a calm or a head-wind are the most annoying things to a sailor, in primitive times they used to try supernatural means to raise wind or turn one in their favor...

Here is a tale about changing the wind by prayer.

There was once an old fisherman who went fishing every evening in a small boat he had bought. Often, when he reached his fishing grounds the wind veered and he had it dead against him on the homeward trip. That annoyed him for he had either to row back to port or wait for the wind to drop.

One day when he had the wind dead against him as he wanted to go fishing, he began to curse, then suddenly remembered his wife's advice and said "My old woman told me to pray to God to change the wind, so that's what I'll do".

So he knelt down in his boat and prayed. The wind did not change till he reached the fishing-grounds. He thanked God for his belated help, however, and promised him a mug of cider when they met.

He threw his boom overboard and put down his lines. Right away he found a shoal of fish and caught as many as he wanted. But when he hoisted sail to leave he found the wind dead against him. So he thought, "If God hadn't changed the wind, I'd have it astern now. If my old woman hadn't told me to pray to God to change the wind it would be still in the north-east and I could easily return to harbor. As it is, its in the south-west, and I'll never get home."

He kept on tacking, and by beating to windward he managed at last to enter harbor. When he got home he told his wife: "I had a bad time getting home today and it's all your fault. I had the wind against me on the way out, after I had prayed to God to make it change as you advised. It changed once I got to the fishing grounds, so I was in the wrong both ways, coming and going. I promised to buy him a mug of cider, but the way I feel, I won't give him a glass of water."

"What do you expect? Since he died his son has been in charge, and he doesn't know the ropes so well as his poor old father. He only did it as a joke. If his dear old father were still in command, he wouldn't have played tricks on a fisherman."

"What do you mean, you old fool?" replied her husband, "It is his son who is dead, unfortunately. If he were alive he would have done a better job than his father, who is in his dotage and doesn't know what he is doing."

"You are right", said his wife, "It is the old one who has done the damage. Next time pray to St. Clement, my dear. He is the saint of the wind and waves, he's more use to you than God."

"You're crazy, old woman. You always have too much faith in those saints. I'd sooner believe in a mug of cider, that would do me more good than all that crowd I don't know from Adam. Give me a sou and I'll go out and drink one."

It is an established fact that gods, some supreme and some minor, ruled the winds and that sometimes each individual wind was a deity or at least an individual being. To obtain favorable winds, sacrifices and prayers were offered up. With the coming of Christianity gods gave way to saints, who took over their attributes. Some saints took the place of the wind and sea-gods and were invoked by sailors with the same superstitious rituals which had been used before. This happened also at sea, as the following example shows: "The weather was calm, but the wind was against us. The Portuguese crew prayed before their statue of St. Anthony for a good wind. But their prayers had no effect, and the sailors, who were impatient and accustomed to treating their statue cavalierly, seized it with the intention of tying it to the mast as a means of forcing the saint to obey. Just as the ropes were made ready, the captain took pity on the saint and spoke up for him, promising he would send the good wind without being forced. So the statue was taken back to its usual place. But as St. Anthony remained deaf to their prayers, the captain gave in and ordered the statue to be tied to the mast. This was done, and the ropes gradually tightened round the saint, who thus suffered martyrdom. The statue before which all had knelt the day before was left tied to the mast and exposed to ridicule and insult. Every day an extra rope was tied around the saint to increase his sufferings. In the end the wind veered in the right direction, so the sailors released St. Anthony, and carried him respectfully to his normal place, thanking him for his help but also reproaching him for his stubbornness, which had forced his devotees to use violence on him and show a lack of proper respect."

French pirates must have borrowed this custom from the Portuguese: "Combalen had made several voyages on Portuguese ships and from these religious fanatics had adopted the belief that St. Anthony was the sole possessor of the sack of Aeolus and should always be invoked when a wind was needed. When the need arose, François always asked for the saint's protection in the same strange way. He stroked the little ivory image of the saint which wore around his neck, and dipped it in the sea."

In classical times magicians were thought to have the winds at their beck and call by means of spells. This belief seemed to gain strength in the Middle Ages. In Scandinavia it was so firmly-rooted that it lasted into the 19th century.

Odde, the Danish ruler of the waves, was said to have crossed the sea without a ship, raised up tempests by magic and by his spells made the swords

of the Danes shine and sparkle like fire.

Oläus tells that Eric, king of Sweden, was a powerful magician and on such familiar terms with evil spirits that the wind would blow from the direction in which he turned his hat. Thus he was nicknamed *Ventosos Pileus* or Wind-Hat:

Sir Walter Scott reported that this belief existed in comparatively recent times in the Shetlands: one of his characters says that he doesn't believe something any more than he believes old wives' tales about King Eric, who could change the wind by turning the point of his hat where he wished. Other folk-tales preserve the idea of the magic hat, but here it is a gift from to Devil to those who have sold themselves to him. In a Norwegian tale the captain makes a pact with the devil, who promises to give him fair voyages. Wherever he goes he has a favorable wind where he wants it. Indeed the still-currents expression "a hatful of wind" still preserves King Eric's memory.

In the 17th century the Indians of Vinland used to sell wind to sea-captains becalmed off their coast. According to Grimm they handed over a ball of string tied with three knots.

Oläus wrote in much the same way of the well-established trade in wind operated by Nordic magicians. The Finns used to do a similar deal with ships held up by contrary winds. For payment in cash they gave the sailor a magic cord with three knots. They warned the sailors that after untying the first knot they would have fair and favorable winds, after the second a stronger wind, but after the third they would have so violent a gale that they would not be able to keep a look-out, take in sail or man the helm.

In the 17th century the people of Northern Sweden still thought that Lapp magicians could summon up a calm, a wind or a storm. One traveller reported thus: "Amongst the many spells used by sorcerers of Lappland is one which can halt a ship in full sail. For this they use a handkerchief knotted in three places, which they give to their customers. When the first knot is untied, there is a mild temperate wind. If a stronger one is needed, the second is untied. But if the third should be undone, there is a terrible storm. It is said that this custom of selling wind is commonplace in that land and that the least important sorcerers have this power, provided the wind needed is already there and simply needs stirring up.

Another author relates that the effectiveness of the handkerchief depended on the time of the magician's birth. He had complete power over the wind prevailing at that time, thus one magician controlled the wind another a contrary one, so that one could speed vessels on their way while another could stop them

dead.

This power could be neutralised by a means mentioned by Pliny: "The only device for counteracting this spell is to spread about the unclean flux of women, the odor of which is intolerable to spirits."

Wind sellers occur in Scottish folklore. One old Scotswoman was approached by a sailor who wanted to cross from Kintyre to Ireland. She gave him two cords each with three knots. When he untied the first he had a fine breeze, the second brought him a fresh wind, the third a gale. On his return voyage to Kintyre he only used two knots of the second cord.

In the Shetlands Sir Walter Scott came across an old witch who made her living by selling favorable winds to the men of Stromney.

Colin de Plancy writes that this power of controlling the winds was contained in an amulet made from the jawbone of a fish inscribed with six characters which initiates could read as "Thor hafot".

This belief in the special powers of magicians was found outside Europe and in the New World. The *Relations des Jésuites du Canada* (1636) says that amongst the Huron Indians were men who earned their living by controlling the winds. Another source says that a magician amongst the natives of Freshwater Bay kept the winds in a bag, like Aeolus, and used certain spells to make them obey him.

Marco Polo relates that on Socotra there were sorcerers who could make the wind blow and force back to port a ship which had been sailing with a breeze behind it.

When there were no magicians or priests people were not completely helpless against the wind. A wide range of countries provides examples of devices used by ordinary sailors or passengers.

Poggio, a famous Florentine who described the voyage made by Nicolo di Conti to the Indies, tells the following story, whose truth he vouches for. A ship was suddenly becalmed, and its nakuda or captain feared that the wind would be long in springing up again, to the disadvantage of himself and his crew. So he had a table prepared at the foot of the mast and a pan of glowing charcoal placed on it. Then he began his spell, mainly directing it at the god Muthiam, the lord of evil spirits. The crew watched, frozen with fear. Suddenly an Arab sailor was seized by a terrible frenzy. He cried that a demon had taken possession of him and entered into his very bones. He screamed, jumped, ran about the ship and then came to the table and ate a piece of glowing charcoal without noticing the heat. Then he said he had a terrible thirst and needed the blood of a rooster to quench it. They went to the chicken-coop, where a few roosters were always kept for such emergencies, and brought him one. He killed it and sucked its blood. Then he grew calmer and asked what was wanted of him "Give us the wind you are holding prisoner", said the captain. "I'll give it to you within three days, and I'll promise it will be favorable. It will come from that direction and take you to your chosen port." With those words the Arab sank down on the deck, half-dead and without the slightest recollection of what he had said and done. After three days the promised wind returned and the ship reached its destination.

In Brittany, when a calm falls, it is enough to whistle for a wind, and old fishermen says it does not delay long. Sometimes whistling can be followed by a prayer to Saint Clement, master of the wind and waves. If the saint is slow to provide a breeze, he is sworn at and called a clown!

Another story tells that St. Clement, master of the winds, taught a captain the art of summoning the winds by whistling.

Another story gives another source for this method: one day a nobleman who had gone for a sail in a fisherman's boat was suddenly becalmed, and the ship, instead of making progress, drifted astern, carried by the current. Both the noble and the fisherman were annoyed. To while away the time the fisherman started to whitle, whereupon the North-West Wind sprang up and carried them to their destination.

The fisherman thanked the North-West Wind and presented him with a bottle of wine, which North-West Wind swallowed at a gulp, for he was thirsty. The fisherman gave him another, which he put in his pocket.

Then the fisherman told the nobleman: "Without Master North-West Wind you wouldn't be here now. You ought to give him something for his trouble. »

Reluctantly the noble took out his purse and gave North-West Wind a gold coin. But the latter refused it because it was given unwillingly, and departed.

Since then winds have almost always answered he prayers of sailors who whistle for them but always ignore the pleas of noblemen.

St. Clement is not the only saint who answers sailors' whistles.

In one of his novels Eugène Sue tells of a sailor who cries "Quick, St. Anthony!" in accordance with sailors' custom.

When there is no wind, the sailors of Tréguier think that St. Anthony, patron saint of the wind, is asleep or angry. To wake him up they swear by him and (as he has forbidden anyone to whistle at sea) whistle with might and main. They say it is the only way to break a calm and raise a wind.

In a calm, Asturian fishermen whistle softly for a wind.

In Northern Scotland sailors whistle, softly at first, to raise the wind. A Scottish proverb alludes to it: "Blaw the wind ne'er sae fast, it will lown at the last."

The Annamites have the same custom—such a powerful device must be used cautiously and never overdone.

In Upper Brittany when someone begin to whistle in a strong breeze, he is told to stop before he summons up a storm.

In Lower Brittany old salts never whistle in foul weather for fear of making it worse.

People who hire out boats in Scarborough tell their customers not to whistle, and the reason is given thus by old sailors: "We only whistle when the wind is asleep, and then it starts blowing." In Norway whistling at sea is thought to cause gales.

When a French ocean-going ship with wind aft met another ship on an opposite course, an old broom was thrown in the path of the other vessel. This was done to ensure that the French ship would always have the wind astern and the other a head wind. Hamburg sailors had the same custom.

Sailors from Pomerania who want a good wind throw a broom in the fire, with the handle pointing in the direction which they want the wind to come. If a head-wind will not drop, an old broom without a handle must be thrown overboard to turn the wind around. But this device must be used with discrimination, as one can never tell the force of the new wind. One might get a full gale which could wreck many ships. Hence the quarrels and abuse which are caused when a broom is cast in front of a vessel with a good wind behind it.

Storms

When a storm is at its height, there appears in the blackness, nobody knows why, that circle of bluish light which old Spanish sailors call "el ojo de la tempestad".   Sailors call it the "eye of the storm", as if they really saw a fierce storm-god like a patch of light in the middle of the sky, surrounded by darkness. This arises from a type of nature—image and from a widespread belief that gods and evil spirits preside over these disturbances and sometimes show themselves to the eye of the beholder.

Naar stormen er störst, kiendes Styremandens konst best. (Danish: It is the storm which shows the helmsman's skill.)

La borasca se conosse sul viso del mariner. (Venetian: The squall shows on the face of the sailor).

A tempu di tempesta, ogni tintu pirtusu e portu. (Sicilian: Any port in a storm.)

In tempo di borasca, ogni tavola basta. (Venetian: In a squall any plank will do.)

Vuti di marinaru duranu quantu la tempesta. (Sicilian: A sailor's promises last as long as the storm.)

Vutu di marinaru e juramentu di jucaturi. (Sicilian: A sailor's promises

181

and a gambler's oaths.)

    Vows made in storms are forgotten in calm. (English.)

    Danger passé

    Saint moqué.

    Passato il pericolo

    Cabbato il santo.

(French and Italian respectively: When the danger is passed the saint is mocked.)

    The danger past, God forgotten. (English.)

    Once on shore

    We pray no more. (English.)

    The sailor thinks of Allah only when the storm blows. (Arab.)

    Sailors from the Charente believe that a storm will last three, six or nine days. This seems to recall similar superstition about number of waves.

In Finistère people think that a storm will only end when the corpses which defile the sea have been cast up on shore.

At night Cornish fishermen avoid places where ships have been wrecked. The souls of drowned men are said to haunt them, crying out to the living. At certain times of the year, and especially before storms, these cries are often heard. More than one fisherman has said they called out to him by name.

Some believe that dead men stir up the wind and the waves and that they rise from their watery graves to warn of foul weather. On the Ile de Sein the inhabitants close their doors when a storm is expected, foretold by will-o'-the-wisps and strange whistling noises.

In ancient times people used to think that a storm was preceded by the coming of the shades of shipwrecked men lamenting their lack of decent burial.

A few days before great storms the inhabitants of the Ile de Sein used to hear a chorus of wails and lamentations rise up into the air. Sometimes a piercing scream of supplication would be heard above the rest. Disaster would befall to those who ignored this warning, for foul weather was not far off.

On the coast of Scotland crowds of ghosts were said to come up out of the sea before a tempest, the ghosts of sailors wrecked on a rock with their ships and so denied Christian burial. The waves which break over this rock carry the sobs and groans of the dying men. White patches on the rock look like the ghosts of the unburied dead come to haunt that awesome spot at midnight.

Ghosts ships have been sighted a fair number of times, sometimes before the storm they foretell, sometimes while it is at its height.

Near Prince Edward Island people say that when a storm is brewing a ball of fire rises out of the sea near the position of a wrecked vessel, swells up into a blazing ship and disappears.

English sailormen do not like to see a cat unusually playfull. They regard it as a sign of a gale to come and say "The cat has a gust of wind in his tail."

In Lancashire they draw the same conclusion when they see a cat running around the house, and in Ireland when a cat stretches itself with its paws together. Cats were believed to be used by witches who raised up storms.

A dead hare aboard used to be seen as certain portent of a gale. In Cornwall a white hare was said to have been seen on the quayside before a storm.

Once there was a Norwegian witch whose husband was a sailor. When a storm approached, she always turned into a crow and perched on the rigging of her husband's ship, croaking "We shall have a storm."

When the coast of Cornwall is threatened by a gale, the bells of the Lord of Bottreaux can be heard ringing far below the waves. Many years ago this lord wanted to present the people of Boscastle with a ring of bells as large as those of Tintagel. He loaded them onto a ship which had almost reached Boscastle when its helmsman wanted to ring a peal on the bells in thanksgiving for a safe voyage. The captain said that it was all due to the strength of his stout ship, and that there would be plenty of time to thank God when they landed. At this a violent gale blew up, the ship was smashed to pieces, and only the helmsman survived to tell the tale.

Around St. Malo people believe that the souls of sailors who have died without the rites of the church and without masses said for the repose of their souls, return during storms to haunt the relatives.

A parallel example comes from America: in Fenimore Cooper's "The Pilot" terrible cries are heard in a storm, which are explained as those of drowned sailors.

Various races have personified storms, sometimes as a god or spirit which needs to be propitiated.

Sea-storms had their own temple in Rome, put up by L. Cornelius Scipio in 259 B.C. near the Porta Capena.

The Greeks called whirlwinds and storms the Harpies. In the *Odyssey* they are always treated as storm goddesses.

In Scandinavian Mythology tempests were likened to birds. In the Saga of Frithiof the hero says: "Brothers, the weather will be rough. I can hear the storm beating its wings afar off... It flaps its wings and with wild fury rushes into the sea or hurtles in the form of a whirlwind up to the very home of the gods". In the same saga Frithiof hurls two boar-spears, one of which pierces the breast of the "black eagle of the tempests".

The Greeks represented storms as a battle between winds, clouds, waves and mountains. A song has survived in which the clouds reproach the sea and ask it to cease its insolence. Three clouds pass through the sky, one bearing fine rain, another hail and the third, the mightiest, battles with the sea.

In Lithuanian folklore the wind and the water are two giants who fight each other.

In the mythology of the Dakota tribe the great Haokah personifies the storm. The four winds were the ring he used to make thunder.

In Vedric hymns the gods of the tempest move the clouds in fury over the sea.

Amongst the Quiché tribe the mysterious creator deity is Huakan. This word has no meaning in their language, but it is believed that they borrowed it from the ancient language of Haiti. From that source the word *hurricane* and its counterparts entered European languages to signify the dreaded Caribean storm.

Sometimes evil spirits took advantage of the absence of the supreme deity to stir up the sea without his permission. The deeds of Neptune are well documented in Homer, and something similar is related in the folklore of the Pacific.

One day Hiro, great pacifier of the waves, fell asleep in one of the deepest waves. Whilst he was asleep, a hurricane blew on a ship carrying some of his friends. The intervention of Hiro recalls Neptune coming to the aid of the fleet of Aeneas.

In classical times storms, especially the worst ones, were ascribed to the anger of the gods who presided over the sea. However, other non-marine deities occasionally had the power to raise up tempests, and sometimes lesser gods made use of the absence of the greater to take their revenge by unleashing the winds and the waves. Analogies can be found amongst remote people less advanced than the Greeks of the Heroic Age. According to Nicolas d'Urville the Maoris think that thunderstorms and tempests are caused by the anger of the god Tawaki, and when Nicolas was battered by great gusts of wind in Shuraki Bay the Maoris decided that Towaki had taken a dislike to him.

In the Hervey Islands it is said that two gods insulted by a hero raised up a terrible storm. According to an Ainu song, when the gods of the sea groan and strike their chests with their fans, the result is a storm over the sea.

In Scotland people used to think that tempests pile up when the Nigg or sea-goblin sleeps.

In some places the appearance of mermaids is a sign of foul weather, in others they are described as deities who are benevolent unless offended.

A Norwegian folk-tale tells of a sailor who cut off a mermaid's hand. He was assailed by a violent storm. In a Scottish legend a fisherman caught a mermaid in his net. She tied two knots in it, and darkness came down. When she tied a third, a gale sprang up, but she listened to his pleas and relented, so a calm fell. I a fisherman's oar touches a mermaid, even by accident, a terrible storm results. On the coast of Finistère it is believed that if a sailor sees a mermaid naked, violent winds will stir up the sea. This compares closely with a Norwegian belief that mermaids are a sign of storms.

In Lower Brittany the mermaid's song lashes wind and waves into a gale, a belief also found in classical times.

In general, gods only show their anger at sea in revenge for some misdeed but this does not apply to spirits. Some of these do evil just out of *Schaden-freude*, though luckily they are usually asleep or otherwise engaged. Hence seafarers who pass near their habitations are advised not to do anything which might attract their attention. When the Svanes are on the move they keep silent or recite sacred hymns in a low voice, for a loud noise can draw a tempest down on them. A similar superstition exists amongst Norwegian fishermen and the Indians of North America.

In the Malay archipelago, by contrast, the storm-raisers are enormous giants. At Macassar other giants are employed by the moon to rule the fishes of the sea and to polish sea-shells. Sometimes they mutiny, and their wrath causes terrible tempests. Their breath produces gales, and when these winds drop it is said that some of the giants have fallen asleep face-downwards on the sea-bed.

In the Celebes giants who have taken possession of the sea raise storms when they grow angry and cause shipwrecks when they sneeze.

The Eskimoes tell of the *kayarissats* who paddle a kayak of enormous size. They are skilled in many kinds of magic and quite capable of causing tempests.

In a Chinese tale an iron cat called General Mao appears on the waters, sent by the sea god to stir up a storm.

Popular beliefs of the Middle Ages associate the Devil with all kinds of destructive activities and striking natural phenomena. Thus it is not surprising that legends saw the hand of the Devil in tempests, sometimes describing him as being sighted at the centre of them in person.

According to Mark the Hermit there was a belief in the mediaeval period that devils of the fourth class had the task of stirring up storms and sinking ships.

In the *Golden Legend* a demon boasts of having caused tempest and sent many a ship to the bottom. According to the same source, when the body of St. Stephen was brought on board a ship, demons stirred up the winds and the waves against it.

The author of the Life of Guibert of Nogent describes the Devil as raising a storm. Legend tell that St. Nicolas calmed a tempest which threatened the ship he was sailing on, but not before he had repulsed the Devil himself, who attacked the ship sword in hand.

Centuries ago the Bermudas were known as the Islands of the Devil, as they were thought to be haunted by a storm-demon.

Sir Walter Scott was of the opinion that Scotland, Ireland and wales contained many places where the memory of certain devils was preserved by superstition. Such devils would cause terrible gales if a plowshare so much as touched one of their stones. When the scholar Borlase discovered ancient tombs in the Scilly Isles, he roused the anger of the local people. They attributed the storms from which they suffered at the time to the enmity of the spirits haunting the tumuli investigated by Borlase. Huron Indians say that a particular spirit rules the waters and causes tempests and shipwrecks. The Caribs assigned the same role to a demon named Maboyo. Froberville reports that the devils or evil spirits living in the sunken land of Kassipi are said to raise up terrible storms at sea.

Sea-monsters, servants of the spirits or spirits in their own right, also have this power. In the Swedish folk-tale *The Sons and Daughters of the King* three monsters try to block the progress of a king by stirring up a terrible storm in the path of his ship.

Since classical times, at least amongst barbarian peoples, priestesses similar to witches also possessed great power over the sea.

Sea-witches

The Anglo-Saxons believed that witches were capable of causing storms at sea. This idea was commonplace in the Middle Ages, especially in northern countries. Oddo the Dane, the great sea-raider, was said to be so killed in magic that he passed over the sea without using a boat and often used spells to raise tempests and destroy enemy ships. Instead of fighting them, he used wind and wave to cause their destruction.

One famous Scandinavian sorcerer was reported to brew a magic potion to raise tempests.

In the 16th century whole communities in nordic lands were credited with power over the sea: "It is said that by their spells and enchantments the people of Greenland stir up storms at sea and endanger foreign ships which they wish to plunder."

Many years ago in the Bay of Corrivreckan there was an old witch who had only to wave her handkerchief to raise up a storm and thus destroy a fleet of ships. A Danish prince was bold enough to defy her one day when she was waving it: he was wrecked with all hands. St. Columba was more fortunate: when he was passing through the Wrecken Channel, he was overtaken by a storm. He spoke to his friend St. Kenneth, who heard his cry of distress many miles away, when he was sitting down to breakfast. St. Kenneth ran to the church with only one shoe on and celebrated mass. It was nine o'clock in the morning when he consecrated the host, and at precisely the same time Columba suddenly saw the waves grow calm around his vessel.

Another witch, at the urging of a clan chief who needed her help against a Spanish fleet, went out on a rock with her handkerchief. Every time she waved it a crow flew up with a squall under its wing. The Spanish fleet was totally destroyed.

At the same period similar beliefs are found among Islamic peoples: at the death of the eunuch Yusuf, who had foretold the defeat of Charles V, simple people thought that they could raise or calm storms by uttering spells over his tomb.

During the siege of Algiers by Charles V a witch came to the governor and told him to hold out for nine days. A dreadful storm then arose which wrecked the galleys of the besiegers. In "Macbeth" Shakespeare, a rich source of folklore about the sea, gives his witches the following dialogue, which is doubtless in accordance with contemporary beliefs.

First witch: A sailor's wife had chestnuts in her lap and munch'd, and
munch'd:"Give me' quoth I;
"Aroint thee, witch!" The rump-fed ronyon cries. Her husband's
to Aleppo gone, master o' the Tiger:
But in a sieve I'll thither sail,
And like a rat without a tail,
I'll do, I'll do, and I'll do.

Second witch: I'll give thee a wind.

Firft witch: Thou'rt kind.

Third witch: And I another.

First witch: I myself have all the other
And the very ports they blow,
All the quarters that they know.
I' the shipman's card.
I will drain him dry as hay:
Sleep shall neither night nor day,
Hang upon his pent-house lid;
He shall live a man forbid.
Weary se' nights nine times nine
Shall he dwindle, peak and pine:
Though his bark cannot be lost,

Yet it shall be tempest-tost.

Look what I have.

Second witch: Show me, show me.

First witch: Here I have a pilot's thumb,

Wreck'd as homeward he did come.

At the beginning of the 17th century many witchcraft trials were held in Scotland, at which learned judges condemned witches to death for causing storms, a phenomenon they and many others of their day believed in.

Sir Walter Scott gives some interesting details on this theme. In 1618 Margaret Barclay, wife of Hannibal Dun, burgess of Irvine was falsely accused of theft by her brother- and sister-in-law. She put a curse on her brother-in-law's ship, on which the Provost of Irvine was a passenger, and prayed that the sea might not bear it up and that crabs might devour all on board at the bottom of the sea.

The ship was in fact wrecked, and a vagabond called John Stewart brought the news soon afterwards. As he was reputed a sooth-sayer, he was arrested and testified that one night he had gone to the house of Margaret Barclay some time after the vessel had set sail. He had found Margaret and other women making figures from clay. One of the figures represented the Provost of Irvine and another the ship. Whilst they were at work the Devil appeared in the form of a little black dog. The women and the black dog then went down to the sea and threw the figures into it, whereupon the waves began to rage and roar, becoming as red as the madder in a dyer's vat. When Margaret Barclay was put to the torture she confessed everything and was executed, her remains being burnt.

When King James I sailed to Denmark his fleet encountered a storm which the king thought was the work of evil spirits. A number of warlocks and witches were later brought to trial, accused of seeking to destroy the fleet sent to bring back James's future queen by means of a tempest.

A Scottish witch was said to stir up the waves by throwing a piece of wood into a pot of water and calling on the Devil. In the Shetlands, certain warlocks were said to be able to turn into seals by putting on sealskins. They cast spells over the sea, pursued ships and raised storms. But ships could be saved by throwing a coin into the waves.

At St. Levan in Cornwall visitors used to be shown a block of stone called Madge Figge's Chair, on which the old crone sat to raise up storms.

In English folklore the witch of Fraddam is said to be still floating off the coast in her coffin and is thought to be the cause of many gales.

In the Orkneys and Shetlands belief in the power of witches survived for a long time. In 1642 Marian Peebles was said to have turned into a porpoise and caused the loss of a boat and its five crew.

In 1716 a certain Mr. Hicks and his daughter were accused before an English court of having raised up storms and wrecked ships. Other Devonshire witches were persecuted for the same crime. Magic implements were found in their homes, amongst them a broom handle with a miniature sail.

At Peel in the Isle of Man they tell the story of a witch who filled a bowl with water and declared that the fishing fleet would be lost at sea. All the ships were sunk, so she was shut up in a barrel filled with nails and rolled down a hillside. The spot where this horrible punishment was carried out had formerly been grass-covered, but since then nothing has grown there.

Superstitions

There is a very ancient belief, exemplified in the Bible, that storms are due to the presence aboard a ship of a wrongdoer. It is to be found in the following passage from the Book of Jonah:

"The Lord sent a strong wind over the sea, and a great tempest sprang up. As the vessel was in great danger of sinking, the crew were very much afraid, and each man cried out to his own god for help. And the captain went up to Jonah and said, "How can you possibly sleep at a time like this? Get up, pray to your god for help, and perhaps he will take pity on us and save our lives."

The sailors said to each other, "Let's draw lots to find out who is the cause of our danger." Jonah's name was drawn. Then they were terribly afraid and said: "Why have you done this?" for they knew that he was running away from the Lord. Jonah replied: "Take me and throw me in the sea, so that it calms down, for I know that this great tempest has come because of me." They cried out to the Lord, "We pray you, Lord, don't let the death of this man lead to our destruction, do not punish us because innocent blood has been spilt, for it is all your doing!" Then they took Jonah and threw him in the sea, and the storm calmed down at once."

The Greeks and Romans shared this belief. Cicero writes that in the midst of a storm the companions of Diagoras the atheist said that they deserved this misfortune for allowing him to come on board their ship.

A strange belief, which is possibly based on the idea that every priest is something of a magician, maintains that his presence on board can bring storms. Many attribute the aversion of sailors to priests to the black color of their habits and also to the fact that they rarely enter a house except when somebody is dying.

An English author sees here a link with the idea that Satan, their great enemy, sends storms especially to destroy them.

In the Middle Ages a priest ran the risk of being thrown overboard when a ship was endangered by a storm, as his black habit was regarded as its cause.

When the Jesuits came to Canada in 1635, they were told that they were the cause of a terrible storm which had sprung up.

In the Mediterranean the presence of a monk or priest on board is considered a bad omen. Captains are very reluctant to have them as passengers as they are said to bring bad luck. One story tells of a ship sailing from one Aegean island to another. When a monk took passage on the ship, a storm blew up and although he prayed that it might stop, the crew wanted to throw him overboard to rid the ship of bad luck. The poor man was finally granted one concession— he would only would be thrown overboard if the wind had not dropped in two hours' time. Fortunately the gale blew itself out, and the monk was saved.

Dutch sailors think that squalls are caused by somebody who has not paid his debts, by a passenger who has committed some terrible crime, by a new piece of furniture, a length of cable, a beard or a scowl.

A venerable publication called *France Maritime* provides us with a very characteristic example of a passenger who brings bad luck: in the middle of a storm a sailor on board the *USS President* came up to the ship's officers: "I am the cause of this storm and the same happens to every ship I embark on", he said. "All my misfortunes are caused by the sinful life I have led for many years now. God will only be appeased if I throw myself into the waves". He jumped into the sea a few moments later. The ship docked at Charleston, and when it sailed again for New York another storm sprang up. The crew were unanimous that the ship would be lost unless all the belongings of the missing sailor were thrown into the sea. A Scotsman threw them over the side and prayed that the sinful sailor might be forgiven, and that God might calm the storm now that the sacrifice was complete. The crew took heart again, and the storm gradually died down. However, another storm sprang up a few days later, and the sailors looked for some item of the missing man's property which might still be on board. They found an old shoe belonging to him and threw it into the waves.

Certain actions were absolutely forbidden on board a ship, for example cutting one's hair when the weather was fine. Whilst one's hair was sometimes offered to the gods, this only happened in extreme cases and was always the last thing sacrificed to the gods of storms by sailors in danger of shipwreck. Cutting one's hair during fine weather was therefore contrary to all religious customs and amounted to tempting Providence and bringing down a storm on one's ship.

The same applied to nails, which were only to be cut only when one was in danger of shipwreck. Nails were damaged and torn when people hung onto rocks, so they were only cut when a ship was in danger at the same time as one tied one's hair in a knot. Cutting them when no storm threatened risked the anger of Neptune and Boreas. References to cutting of hair can be found in the *Twelfth Satire* of Juvenal, and Propertius refers to nail-cutting in one of his elegies.

There is a story which says that the passengers of a ship carrying a petition drawn up by American settlers inspired by Cotton Mather believed that the vessel was in danger of being sunk by a storm and demanded that the document be thrown overboard.

When a member of the crew dies on board a ship, foul weather is thought to follow. Traces of this ancient superstition can be seen in the following story about St. Mary Magdalene from the *Golden Legend:* when sailors saw a woman die in childbirth during a storm they said, "Let's throw this body into the sea before we all die together, for the storm will not die down as long as it stays on board."

An example from Shakespeare shows this point being discussed:

First sailor: Sir, your queen must overboard: the sea works high, the wind is loud and will not lie till the ship be cleared of the dead.

Pericles: That's your superstition.

First sailor: Pardon us, sir; with us at sea it hath been still observed, and we are strong in custom. Therefore briefly yield her, for she must overboard straight.

Prince Radziwill reports a curious incident in his account of his journey to Jerusalem. In Egypt he had bought two mummies, one male and one female, and had them put secretly in a box which was taken on board his ship in Alexandria in preparation for his return to Europe. Only two servants knew his secret... "When we were at sea a storm sprang up several times with such great violence that the captain despaired of saving his ship. Everyone expected to be shipwrecked before long. A Polish priest in the prince's entourage said prayers suited to the sad occasion, whilst the prince and his suite joined in. But the priest said he was troubled by two ghosts, a man and a woman, both black and hideous, who threatened him with death. At first it was thought that fear and danger had disturbed his sanity. When calmer weather came he seemed easier in his mind, but when the storm blew up again he was more troubled than before. He had no peace until the two mummies were thrown overboard, which he had not seen and which neither he nor the captain knew were on board."

Plutarch writes that the druids believed souls of great men to be so closely attached to the world that they could not leave it without upsetting the balance of nature. When Demetrius accompanied Claudius to britain a great storm sprang up, and the druids told him that a void had been left by the departure of some great man's soul. When great men die, their death stirs up winds and storms (Camille Flammarion, *Histoire du ciel*).

Several legends link storms with birds: "A bird nests continually on that rock, hatching out its seven eggs, whilst it is in its nest the sea is calm. But if it goes away the sea is so troubled that nobody can cross it without being shipwrecked. There is another great bird which continually tries to steal the eggs of the one mentioned before and get into its nest. When the robbed bird sees its nest despoiled, it flies off in great distress. This bird is also distressed by the blood of a lamb. *(Le violer des histoires romaines.)*

Some natives of Tierra del Fuego who came on board the *Beagle* on Darwin's voyage predicted rough weather because the ship's surgeon had killed some seabirds.

The fishermen of Rosehearty in Scotland all agree that a wedding causes a storm along the coast. The favorite time for weddings is just after the herring fishing season, that is, from September to January.

Violent upheavals of the sea are also linked by popular superstition with sexual relations, licit or illicit. "When a man takes his godmother to wife, each time they have carnal knowledge of one another there is a thunderstorm or a tempest over sea or land" *(Evangile des Quenouilles)*. In a novel by E. Sue an old Breton captain says there will be a storm because one of the men from his village has married his godmother. The sea off Saint-Jean-du-Doigt in Finistère is lashed to a fury whenever it catches sight of a woman or girl.

A peculiar Breton legend tells that storms were raised for the convenience of a saint. The old people of Clohars-Carnouet, say that many years ago St. Maudé used to come every year on his day (26th November) to his chapel by the sea-shore in their parish. A gale of wind from the north used to take him from

196

beloved Ireland to the coast of Brittany. When he arrived at Loc-Maudé, his chapel, he tied his horse to a piece of ashlar which still stands in that spot, took care of the pilgrims needs and gave them his blessing. Then he made in great haste for Le Pouldhu and visited his friend St. Julian. Hardly had he returned from this visit when the winds veered right around to the south, enabling him to reach home before nightfall.

Several passages from the *Golden Legend* or popular religious works show saints intervening, sometimes in person, to calm the waves either during their life or after their death.

One day some sailors in danger of death prayed with bitter tears to St. Nicolas: "Nicolas, servant of God, if it's true what we have heard, grant us your help. » A man appeared who looked like St. Nicolas and said, "Here I am, are you calling me?" He began to help them handle the ship, and the storm ceased. When they came to his church those who had not seen the statue before recognised it as that of their rescuer *(Golden Legend)*.

During a sea-voyage St. Nicolas once warned the captain of a terrible storm which the Devil would stir up. The storm was so dreadful that all the passengers thought they would killed. But St. Nicolas prayed for them, drove off the demon who threatened their lives and made the sea calm again. He has worked miracles like this several times, which is why seafarers take him as their patron saint and protector.

The Greeks regard St. Nicolas as the master of the sea and call him the Christian Neptune. They say he leaves port in a storm and walks over the waves in boots made of sea-weed to guide mariners to safety with his invisible arm.

In Russia St. Nicolas was the patron saint of the nobility, children and sailors, and he had many devotees around the White Sea. All his ikons depict him looking down anxiously on the storms of the White Sea.

Whilst on his journey to Jerusalem Chateaubriand's ship was beset by a storm, and he observed that prayers were said to the Virgin Mary and to the saints: "At three o'clock the sails were reefed and a little lamp hung before a picture of the Blessed Virgin in the captain's cabin. The storm was at its height. Our Austrian captain started praying in the midst of torrents of rain and claps of thunder. We prayed for ourselves and for sailors "buried in the holy sea."

The Chevalier d'Arvieux relates that once in a terrible storm "all those lying down got up instantly, praying for mercy; on all sides one heard nothing but "Jesus, Mary!"... Captain Martin took a crucifix, summoned his crew and directed their handling of the ship. I was asked to read the Gospel according to St. John. This I did with the aid of the lightning, by whose light the sailors also went about their work."

The custom of saying prayers at sea goes back to remote antiquity. It continued throughout the Middle Ages, and on one occasion Columbus sent some of his crew ashore to go in procession to a chapel. These Castilians went dressed only in their shirts, in accordance with a vow they had made.

In the days of Henry VIII Captain Arthur made a vow to Our Lady of Walsingham to the effect that if, it pleased God to save him from danger he would eat neither fish nor flesh until he had made a pilgrimage to her shrine. Admiral Lord Howard allowed him to go ashore immediately after the storm.

One sailor made a very strange vow: if he were saved, he promised to seek the ugliest and most wanton girl in all Brittany and marry her. It is said that he made a careful search and when he found the girl who fitted this description best, made her his wife.

Mackenzie writes that when he was in North America the owner of the canoe in which he was travelling said he would never use it again because he had made a solemn vow to this effect whilst negotiating some dangerous narrows.

The formula used by the priests of the Middle Ages to calm storms has come down to us. When they had spoken the words they pointed a cross towards the four corners of the heavens and sprinkled holy water about.

This art formed part of the education of every Viking.

In Sir Walter Scott's *The Pirate*, Norna uses a Nordic spell to calm the winds.

Such beliefs existed in Islamic countries, in the Pacific and in the Arctic regions of the North. Some Moors returning from Sofala in a storm, approached Cabral and asked him whether he had on board a magician who could calm it down.

"Before setting sail the *raïs* (captain) never fails to visit one of their most famous Marabouts, to consult him about his voyage and ask for his prayers. The Marabout gladly agrees to take care of the matter, at the same time giving him a fine sheep to sacrifice at sea, such offer being made only when there is a great storm or some other extremity..."

When a storm places them in great danger they take this sheep and without skinning it, cut it in half while it is still alive, all the time observing complete silence. When that is done they take the portion with the head and throw it into the sea over the right-hand side of the vessel. Then they throw the other half over the left-hand side. Whilst so doing they make strange grimaces, turn their heads from side to side, perform many strange antics and mutter confused words which I do not think it necessary to report here.

It sometimes happens that this first sheep (which they esteem so highly because of the Marabout from which it came) has been sacrificed in vain. In such case they take another sheep from amongst a number they have on board for this purpose, believing that some fault in the first one had prevented the success of their hopes. They then sacrifice the second sheep in the same strange manner as has been described above. But if they meet with no success a second time, they start again and often sacrifice up to a dozen sheep".

If the prayers of Arab mariners beset by storms were not granted, they beat their Christian galley-slaves and forced them to offer up prayers to the Virgin Mary and St. Nicolas.

An example from an old French dictionary seems to indicate that sailors used to utter certain rythmic cries or used certain chants when foul weather threatened: *Celeama, clamor nauticus, quem.* The dictionary does not state whether this is a prayer or a lamentation.

It appears that payers and lamentations were not the only things uttered by sailors under such circumstances: Captain Cook reported that during storms he heard their voices above the fury of the wind and waves shouting dreadful curses and that it is impossible to imagine the weird swear words produced by their rage.

A merchant from Mecca once told Niebuhr *(Travels through Arabia)* that when in danger of death at sea one day he fixed a piece of paper with cabalistic writings to the mast, with the result that the storm died down immediately.

According to *Les Admirables secrets du grand Albert* coral is extremely effective against storms and perils of the sea. An old English text relates that in the 16th century coral was thought to save ships endangered by storms. In classical times two bones from the head of a fish of the species *Scioena aquila* made an effective amulet against tempest but only if they had been given or borrowed, not bought. Magicians in the Middle Ages claimed that peonies picked under certain mysterious conditions were a cure for storms.

Greek sailors beset by storms threw small pieces of bread into the waves and said prayers to calm the waves. Russian sailors used to throw overboard cakes made of flour and butter to appease the evil spirit who stirred up the waters of the White Sea.

A Chinese legend tell that when an honest magistrate accepted an ink-stone as a bribe, a storm sprang up. His conscience was troubled, so he threw it into the sea. At once the storm abated, and there rose from the waves an island known nowadays as the Island of the Ink-Stone. There is a variant of this story in which the mandarin reproaches the gods for ill-treating a man who had always done his duty. He throws the stone into the water, where it becomes an island.

By throwing some valuable object into the sea it was hoped to appease the spirit who had unleashed the storm. This custom was common amongst Arab sailors of the Middle Ages.

These sacrifices were not always enough and sometimes the irritated gods demanded human victims. In this case it was the person whose presence on board had caused the storm who was thrown over the side, but sometimes one person volunteered to sacrifice himself for the common good.

In a Swedish folksong, Adeline, who has come aboard against the captain's wishes, throws overboard her golden casket, her grey horse and various other valuables. As the storm still will not abate, she asks the captain to tell her fiancée that she will celebrate their marriage in the sea and jumps into the water.

When a Japanese folklore hero was crossing the sea a violent storm sprang up and his ship was in danger of sinking. His wife realized that the sea spirits were demanding a human sacrifice. She threw into the raging waters eight reed mats, then eight made of leather, then eight made of silk. Then she herself leaped into the waves and disappeared from sight. The storm stopped immediately.

Printed by
Officine Grafiche
de Aldo Garzanti Editore s.p.a.
Milano

Printed in Italy